First Look at...
Quattro Pro for Windows

Lisa Rosner

Mitchell McGRAW-HILL
New York St. Louis San Francisco Auckland Bogotá Caracas
Lisbon London Madrid Mexico City Milan Montreal New Delhi
San Juan Singapore Sydney Tokyo Toronto

Mitchell **McGRAW-HILL**
Watsonville, CA 95076

First Look at Quattro Pro for Windows

Copyright © 1993 by **McGRAW-HILL, Inc.** All rights reserved. Printed in the United States of America. Except as permitted under the United States Copyright Act of 1976, no part of this publication may be reproduced or distributed in any form or by any means, or stored in a database or retrieval system, without the prior written permission of the publisher.

2 3 4 5 6 7 8 9 0   DOH DOH   9 0 9 8 7 6 5 4 3

ISBN 0-07-053830-1

Sponsoring editor: Erika Berg
Editorial assistant: Jennifer Gilliland
Technical reviewer: Jeff Mock, Diablo Valley College
Director of production: Jane Somers
Production supervisor: Leslie Austin
Project manager: Carol Dondrea, Bookman Productions
Interior designer: Renee Deprey
Cover designer: Janet Bollow
Cover photo: W. Warren/**West**light
Compositor: Christi Payne Fryday, Bookman Productions
Printer and binder: R. R. Donnelley & Sons

Library of Congress Card Catalog No. 92-64184

Information has been obtained by Mitchell McGraw-Hill from sources believed to be reliable. However, because of the possibility of human or mechanical error by our sources, Mitchell McGraw-Hill, or others, Mitchell McGraw-Hill does not guarantee the accuracy, adequacy, or completeness of any information and is not responsible for any errors or omissions or the results obtained from use of such information.

This book is printed on acid-free paper.

Contents

Preface   viii

LESSON 1 — Introducing Windows   1

Objectives   1
How to Use This Book   1
The Keyboard and the Mouse   2
What Is Windows?   4
Starting Windows   6
Understanding the Desktop and the Windows   6
    Moving Around the Desktop • Moving Around the Menu Bar • Resizing, Opening, and Closing Windows
Starting a Program   12
Formatting a Disk   14
Exiting a Windows Program   15
Exiting Windows   15
Summary of Commands   16
Review Questions   17
Hands-On Exercises   18

LESSON 2 — Exploring Quattro Pro for Windows   20

Objectives   20
Starting Quattro Pro for Windows   20
The Spreadsheet Notebook   22
Moving Around the Spreadsheet Notebook   23
    Moving Among Pages • Moving Within a Page
Editing Cell Information   25
Entering Data: Labels, Values, and Formulas   26
    A Shortcut for Entering Data • Formulas Using Cell Addresses
Deleting Cell Contents   28
The SpeedBar   28
The Menu Bar   30
    Choosing a Menu Command • Menu Terminology

The Title Bar   31
Saving Your Spreadsheet Notebook   32
Closing a Notebook and Displaying a New, Blank Notebook   33
Exiting Quattro Pro for Windows   33
Summary of Commands   34
Review Questions   35
Hands-On Exercises   36

LESSON 3   Creating a Notebook   38

Objectives   38
Creating a Spreadsheet Notebook   38
Selecting a Block with the Mouse   39
Copying a Block with the Mouse   40
Using Formulas   42
Relative and Absolute Cell Addresses   43
   An Easy Way to Enter Cell Addresses in Formulas
Using SpeedSum to Add Up Columns   45
Introducing Functions   45
Changing the Display of Values   46
   Object Inspector Menus
Changing Column Width with the SpeedBar   49
Deleting a Block   50
Summary of Commands   51
Review Questions   52
Hands-On Exercises   52

LESSON 4   Editing a Notebook   55

Objectives   55
Opening a Notebook   55
Changing Values in a Notebook   56
Inserting and Deleting Rows and Columns   57
   Inserting Rows • Inserting Columns • Deleting Rows and Columns
Subtotals: More About Formulas   59
Copying Cell Contents   60
   Copying and Modifying Labels • Copying Numbers • Copying Formulas and Functions
Moving Cell Contents   63
Drawing Lines and Boxes   63
Printing the Active Notebook Page   65

Contents   v

Summary of Commands   66
Review Questions   67
Hands-On Exercises   68

LESSON 5

More Editing, More Functions   70

Objectives   70
Specifying Column Width   71
Using the Keyboard to Select a Block   72
Changing Alignment   73
Combining Currency and Comma Format   73
Using the SpeedSort Button   74
Using the @COUNT, @MAX, and @MIN Functions   76
Using the @PMT Function   77
Creating Links   78
Copying Functions   78
Using the @IF Function   81
Summary of Commands   82
Review Questions   83
Hands-On Exercises   84

LESSON 6

Creating a Database   87

Objectives   87
Designing a Database   87
  Filling a Block with Sequential Values • Assigning Names to Fields
Sorting the Database   92
Locating Records in a Database   94
Extracting Records from a Database   95
Resetting Data | Query   96
Using Point Mode in Dialog Boxes   97
Summary of Commands   98
Review Questions   98
Hands-On Exercises   99

LESSON 7

Creating Graphs   102

Objectives   102
Creating a Graph with the Graph Tool   103
Changing the Graph Type   103
Printing a Floating Graph   104

Creating a Graph Using the Graph Menu   106
   Specifying Series • Editing Series • Adding Text
Viewing a Graph from the Graphs Page   110
Naming a Graph from the Graphs Page   110
Line Graphs   110
Adding Series Labels Using Object Inspector Menus   111
Printing a Graph   114
Summary of Commands   114
Review Questions   115
Hands-On Exercises   116

LESSON 8 Working with Multiple-Page Notebooks   118

Objectives   118
Moving a Block Between Pages   119
   Changing Page Names
Splitting the Screen into Two Windows   122
   Moving Between and Within Windows • Resizing Windows
Using File | Retrieve   124
Dividing a Notebook into Multiple Pages   125
   Using Drag and Drop to Move Blocks • Absolute Cell References with Multiple-Page Notebooks
Defining a Group of Pages   127
Defining Noncontiguous Blocks   128
Using SpeedBar Buttons with Grouped Pages   129
Adding Cell Contents Across Grouped Pages   130
Summary of Commands   131
Review Questions   132
Hands-On Exercises   133

LESSON 9 Printing Notebooks and Graphs   135

Objectives   135
Printing a Multiple-Page Notebook on One Page   135
   Setting Heads and Footers • Centering Text on the Printed Page
Previewing Before Printing   138
   Adjusting Margins • Changing Header Font Attributes • Printing from the Preview Screen
Saving Print Settings   140
Selecting a Multiple-Page Print Block   141
   Printing Notebook Pages Separately • Alignment, Dates, and Page Numbers in Headers and Footers

Creating Headings from Row and Column Labels   144
Printing a Graph from the Graphs Page   145
    Adding Headers and Footers to Graphs
Summary of Commands   146
Review Questions   148
Hands-On Exercises   148

Answers to Review Questions   150

Quattro Pro for Windows Reference and Command Summary   154

Troubleshooting Guide   161

Index   163

Preface

First Look at Quattro Pro for Windows is a self-paced, hands-on tutorial that covers the essential and most commonly used features of Quattro Pro for Windows. This book can be used:

- in a short course on Quattro Pro for Windows
- as a supplement in a microcomputer applications course
- as a supplement in a variety of business courses
- as a self-paced guide to Quattro Pro for Windows

ORGANIZATION

Written in plain English using step-by-step instructions, this book and other books in the First Look Series quickly get the reader "up to speed" with today's popular software packages in a minimum number of pages. Complete with a Command Summary, a helpful Troubleshooting Guide, and a thorough Index, *First Look at Quattro Pro for Windows* makes reference quick and easy.

First Look at Quattro Pro for Windows begins with basic start-up information, then progresses to more advanced features of Quattro Pro for Windows. The following features aid learning in each lesson:

- **Objectives** provide an overview.
- **Step-by-step, hands-on tutorials** guide the reader through specific functions and commands.
- **Screen displays** monitor the reader's progress.
- **Summary of Commands** makes reference quick and easy.
- **Review Questions** reinforce key concepts.
- **Hands-On Exercises** require readers to apply the skills and concepts just learned.

As readers work through *First Look at Quattro Pro for Windows*, they create files that they use in later lessons. These files should be saved on a data disk so they can be easily located and retrieved; instructions for formatting disks

Preface   ix

are given in Lesson One. It is assumed that readers have access to the full-powered software package and all its features.

First Look at Quattro Pro for Windows has two special features that appear throughout the text to help readers master the software.

- **Caution boxes** warn readers about common pitfalls that beginning users encounter and describe how to avoid them.
- Borland's **Object Inspector menus icon** (displayed in the left margin) lets readers know when they should right-click to bring up an Object Inspector menu.

Use the First Look Series for brief and affordable coverage of today's most popular software applications packages.

ACKNOWLEDGMENTS

I would like to thank John Theibault, Lillian Rosner, Henry Rosner, Marianne Rosner, Andrew Rosner, Abbee Goldstein, Mark Rosner, April Jade Rosner, and of course, Alice Rebecca Theibault, all of whose help and encouragement was necessary for this book's completion.

I would also like to thank the following reviewers for their excellent suggestions: Jeff Mock of Diablo Valley College, Curtis Meadow of the University of Maine at Orono, Pamela J. Cox of Johnson County Community College, Jerald Cole of the U.S. Coast Guard Academy, and Marilyn R. Zook of Mt. Hood Community College.

Lisa Rosner
Stockton State College
Pomona, New Jersey

LESSON ONE: Introducing Windows

OBJECTIVES

At the end of this lesson, you will be able to:
- Understand the keyboard and the mouse.
- Start Windows.
- Understand the desktop and the windows.
- Move around the desktop.
- Move around the menu bar.
- Resize, open, and close windows.
- Start a Windows program.
- Format a disk.
- Exit a Windows program.
- Exit Windows.

HOW TO USE THIS BOOK

Borland's Quattro Pro for Windows is a new entry into the Windows spreadsheet market. Although it is based on Borland's earlier spreadsheet program, Quattro Pro for DOS, Borland's CEO, Philippe Kahn, has been widely quoted as saying that the program is more than just an upgrade. Instead it has been completely redesigned from the bottom up. The standard benefits of a spreadsheet program are the ability to carry out calculations and to analyze different scenarios for decision making. Quattro Pro for Windows can do all that, but it also takes full advantage of new features that spreadsheet users have asked for: use of the mouse to move and edit data, shortcuts for selecting frequently used commands, easy formatting of spreadsheet contents, enhanced graphs and charts, a quick and intuitive way to link many spreadsheets together, and presentation-quality spreadsheet printing. *First Look at Quattro Pro for Windows* mirrors Borland's approach by introducing both basic spreadsheet skills and the most innovative features of the program. By concentrating on what is new and improved, *First Look at Quattro Pro for Windows* allows you to acquire a state-of-the-art knowledge of this state-of-the-art spreadsheet.

This book, which is organized into nine lessons, assumes that you are using Quattro Pro for Windows 1.0 and Windows 3.1. The first lesson is a general introduction to Windows 3.1 and to the keyboard and mouse skills you will need for both Windows and Quattro Pro for Windows. The remaining eight lessons are devoted to Quattro Pro for Windows itself. The book assumes that you begin Lessons Two through Nine by starting Quattro Pro for Windows and that you end each lesson by saving your work and exiting the program. I recommend that you do each lesson in the order in which it appears because later lessons build upon skills acquired in earlier ones. Each lesson has a set of review questions in addition to two or three hands-on exercises. The first exercise is designed to test your skills in the topics covered in the lesson. Subsequent exercises are more challenging and require you to apply your skills in more creative ways.

You can save your work on either the computer's hard disk or on a floppy disk. If you use a brand-new floppy disk, it will have to be formatted. Instructions for formatting a disk using Windows 3.1 are given in Lesson One. Lesson Two gives instructions for saving your work on either the hard disk or on a floppy disk in drive A.

Both Windows and Quattro Pro for Windows are very visual and give you as much information on-screen as possible. For that reason you should watch your computer screen carefully as you carry out the instructions in this book. You will also find it helpful to pay close attention to the figures in each lesson. Since, as the saying goes, A picture is worth a thousand words, you will find a single figure more useful than many pages of description. You should be aware, though, that computers can be set up in different ways, which may affect the way programs are displayed on the monitor. If you notice that your computer screen looks very different from the figures in this text, check with your instructor to see if the difference is due to your computer setup.

THE KEYBOARD AND THE MOUSE

If you haven't used a computer before, take time to examine the **keyboard** (see Figure 1-1). Most keys are exactly like typewriter keys and you type on them as you would on a typewriter. Instead of appearing on paper, though, the words you type will appear on the computer monitor.

The keyboard also contains some special keys used only in computer programs: Enter (also called Return in some programs), the function keys (F1, F2, F3, F4, F5, F6, F7, F8, F9, F10), and the arrow keys (←, →,

Lesson 1/Introducing Windows   **3**

IBM PC/XT Keyboard Layout

Enhanced IBM PC/AT Keyboard Layout

Figure 1-1
The keyboard

[↑], [↓]). Other special keys are the [Ctrl], [Esc], [Ins], [Alt], [Del], [Backspace], [Home], [End], [Pg Up], and [Pg Dn] keys.

For most keystrokes, you press the key for the count of 1, as you would on a typewriter. For some commands, though, Quattro Pro for Windows will expect you to press one key while holding down another. In this book, these commands will be written as two keys separated by a hyphen. An example of this is the keyboard command [Alt]-[F3], discussed in Lesson Three. This requires you to first press [Alt], then hold it down while pressing [F3]. To get the feel of this, think of counting 1...2...3. On the count of 1 hold down [Alt], on the count of 2 press [F3], and on the count of 3 release them both.

Most of the features in Quattro Pro for Windows can be selected using the **mouse** as well as the keyboard. In fact, the program has been widely praised for being so easy to use with a mouse. For that reason, *First Look at Quattro Pro for Windows* emphasizes mouse techniques. The mouse is designed to be held comfortably in one hand while being moved along any hard surface. On the top are from one to three buttons and on the bottom is a small ball. You **position** the mouse by moving it (thus rolling the ball) on the desk or computer table until the **mouse pointer** on the screen is correctly placed (see Figure 1-2).

The main mouse techniques that you will need for Windows and Quattro Pro for Windows are **clicking**, **right-clicking**, **dragging**, and **double-clicking**. To *click*, press the left mouse button once and release quickly. To *right-click*, press the right mouse button once and release quickly. When instructed to "press" or "click" the mouse in this book, press the left button unless the right button is specifically mentioned.

NOTE: *If your mouse has three buttons, the left button is the one all the way on the left and the right button is the one all the way on the right. Ignore the one in the middle.*

Figure 1-2
The mouse and mouse pointer

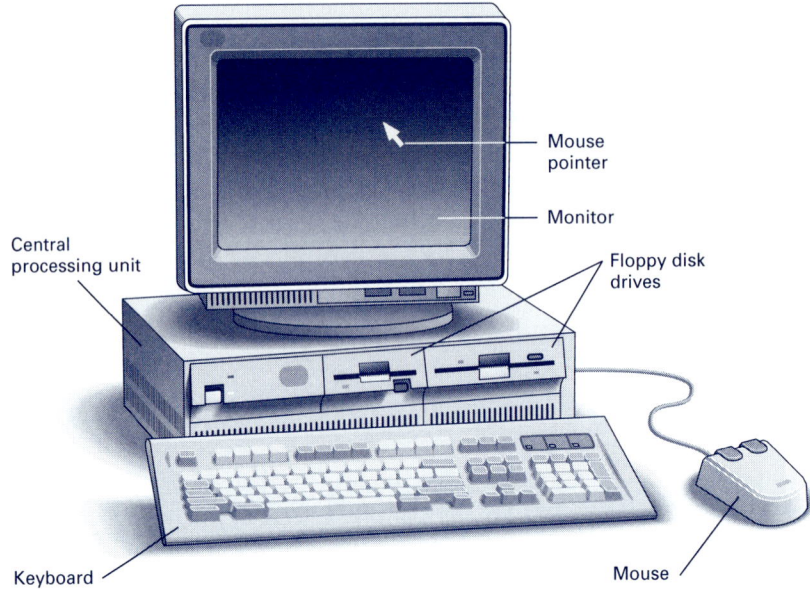

To *drag*, press down on the left mouse button and hold it while moving the mouse, then release it. To *double-click*, quickly press and release the left mouse button twice without moving the mouse. These techniques have different purposes in different programs. Their use in Windows will be explained in more detail in this lesson; their use in Quattro Pro for Windows will be explained in later lessons.

WHAT IS WINDOWS?

Windows is a program that organizes and helps manage the other programs on your computer. It works together with the computer **operating system**, called "MS-DOS." "MS" stands for Microsoft, the company that makes the operating system. "DOS" stands for Disk Operating System.

But what, you may ask, is an operating system? The easiest way to answer that is to say what it does. An operating system keeps the parts of a computer —the monitor, disk drives, processing unit, and the like—running smoothly together. It copies, moves, and deletes files. It understands your commands to start a program as well as your commands to end it. You turn it on when you turn on the switches to your computer and you turn it off when you turn off the switches.

It may help to think of DOS as a reasonably large and intelligent octopus that lives in your computer. Each of its tentacles is attached to a different part of the computer, both the parts that you can see, like the monitor, and those you can't, like the circuitry. Part of the octopus's job is to make sure that all the parts run smoothly together. But the other part is to respond to commands that you give the computer by typing at the keyboard or using the mouse. These commands include housekeeping chores like formatting disks and copying files; they also include starting programs and ending them. To make the metaphor even more complicated, you can think of programs as compact disks and the octopus as a deejay who plays them for you. On a computer that has DOS but not Windows, the octopus is like a deejay with only one CD player and one broadcast microphone. That means you can only command it to "play," or **run**, one program at a time: When you are word processing, you can't use a spreadsheet program, and when you use a spreadsheet program, you can't use a database program.

Even more inconvenient is the fact that the DOS octopus only understands certain commands. Each program generally requires a different command to start; once it has started, each has a different set of commands to carry out specific tasks. Knowing the command for copying a file doesn't tell you anything about how to start a word processing program; knowing how to edit a letter doesn't tell you anything about how to start a spreadsheet program. In fact on many computers, you cannot even find out a list of available programs unless you already know DOS commands: All you will see when you turn on the computer is an almost blank screen displaying the **C prompt** (C:>). This is the sign that the octopus is waiting for a command. Unfortunately if you don't know what command to type, you and the computer can sit staring at each other all day.

Using Windows makes communicating with the octopus much easier. Windows arranges all the programs on your computer so that you can easily see them, and you can start each one with the same mouse techniques. Programs that are specially designed to run from Windows, like Quattro Pro for Windows, use similar techniques to carry out similar tasks. You can also use Windows to run more than one program at a time, though we will not be discussing that technique in this book. If you are interested, check your Windows manual for information on switching between applications.

CAUTION: This lesson is intended to be a brief introduction to those Windows skills that will make it easier for you to use Quattro Pro for Windows. It is not a complete guide to Windows. For more information, check your Windows manual or a textbook such as **First Look at Windows 3.0/3.1** *by Ruth Schmitz (Mitchell McGraw-Hill, 1992).*

STARTING WINDOWS

The programs on a computer, like furniture in a living room, can be arranged in many different ways. Some computers are set up so that Windows starts automatically whenever the computer is turned on. Others display a list, called a **menu**, of available programs and expect you to select Windows from the list. Still others display only the C prompt. If your computer fits any of those descriptions, follow the instructions below to start Windows; if not, consult with your instructor.

1. Turn on the computer. If the Windows logo appears or if the screen resembles Figure 1-3, then Windows has automatically started. Skip to the next section.

2. If a menu with a list of programs, one of which is Windows, appears, follow the instructions on the screen to select it. Usually the instructions will tell you to press a number or letter corresponding to the program you wish to select and then to press [Enter]. If the Windows logo appears or if the screen resembles Figure 1-3, then Windows has started. Skip to the next section.

3. If you see the C prompt (C:>), type **WIN** and press [Enter]. If the Windows logo appears or if the screen resembles Figure 1-3, then Windows has started. Move to the next section.

UNDERSTANDING THE DESKTOP AND THE WINDOWS

Part of the power of Windows comes from its successful mixing of two metaphors, the desktop and the window. When you first start Windows, the **desktop**, Windows' name for the screen background, appears on your monitor. It should look something like Figure 1-3, but because it is easy to rearrange (as you will see), some parts of it may look different. The idea behind the desktop is to simulate your ordinary working environment. If you sat down to work at a real desk, you would probably want to have everything you need conveniently located. Each of the projects you intend to work on might be filed away in a separate drawer; each of the tools you want to work with, such as a calculator or clock, might be on a shelf nearby. The Windows desktop is organized in the same way. Figure 1-3 shows an especially neat and tidy desktop: Each separate computer program you might wish to use is filed away in a box called a **program group**. The box labeled "Windows Applications" contains programs written especially to run with Windows, like Quattro Pro for Windows. The Accessories box contains tools, such as a calculator and a clock.

Figure 1-3
The Windows desktop

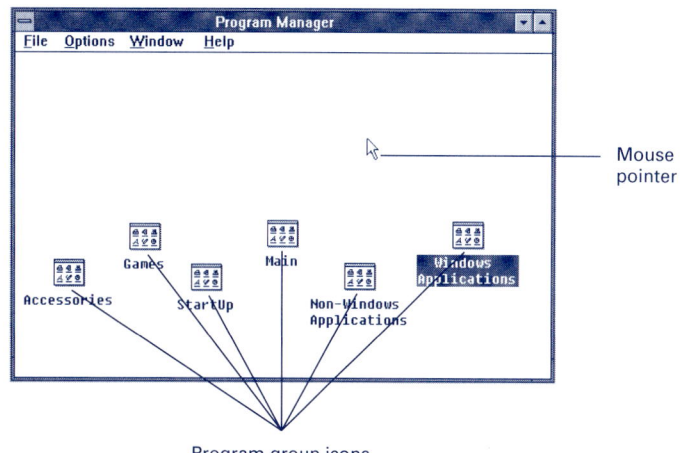

To get at the programs and the tools, you need to understand Windows' other metaphor, the **windows** that give the program its name. Imagine that the windows on your house could be moved and stretched or contracted whenever you wished. You could rearrange them to look into any room, expand them to take up an entire wall, or shrink them until they closed up completely. If you wanted to add a new picture to a wall, you could move the windows out of the way; if you planted a new garden, you could expand the windows on that side of the house to enjoy the view.

You can't do that with real windows. But you can with Windows windows. Each of the program group boxes is really a window, shrunk down to the smallest possible size so that only a picture, called an **icon**, is displayed. You can **restore** each window to full size if you want to see what is in it, **maximize** it until it fills the entire screen, or manually expand or contract each side. In fact the large box you see in Figure 1-3 is itself a window containing the **Program Manager**, the part of Windows that organizes and displays the different programs on your computer. In Figure 1-3 the Program Manager window is displayed full size. Of course, combining the desktop and windows is mixing metaphors, because real desk tops don't have windows in them. But it is a useful mixed metaphor for getting work done on the computer.

Moving Around the Desktop

The easiest way to move around the desktop and carry out tasks in Windows is to use the mouse. The arrow you see on the screen is the mouse pointer in Windows (refer to Figure 1-3). You move the mouse pointer around the desktop by moving the mouse on a flat surface. When you lift the mouse from the surface, the arrow remains stationary. In other words, waving the mouse at the screen will not accomplish anything. This is useful in case, for example, you want to move the arrow all the way across the screen from left to right but reach the end of the flat surface when the arrow is only halfway across. Simply pick up the mouse, move it back to the left edge of the surface, then put it down and move it to the right again. The mouse pointer will not move while the mouse is in the air; it will only move when the mouse has again made contact with the flat surface. Practice moving the mouse pointer until you can comfortably position it anywhere on the screen.

Next, practice *clicking* by moving to each of the program groups in turn and clicking on it.

1. Position the mouse pointer on the Accessories program group icon and click. A menu, called the **Control menu**, will be displayed with various choices. You can choose to Restore the program group window to full-size, Move it, Maximize it, Close it, or select the Next program group icon. You *cannot* choose to change the icon's Size or Minimize it. Those choices are dimmed out, because you cannot change the size of an icon nor make it any smaller than it already is.

2. For now you do not want any of the choices. To remove the menu, click on the background to the icon. The menu will disappear.

3. Click on each of the program groups in turn, then click on the background to close up the menu.

Finally you will practice moving each of the icons within the Program Manager by *dragging*.

1. Position the mouse pointer on the Accessories icon. Press the left mouse button, drag the icon to another part of the Program Manager window, and release the mouse button.

2. Practice dragging each of the icons around the window until you feel comfortable moving icons with the mouse.

3. Move them back to their original positions.

Moving Around the Menu Bar

The **menu bar** looks like nothing more than four words on a line (see Figure 1-4). But it is really four separate menus of commands grouped under convenient headings, File, Options, Window, and Help. To "pull down" the menus so that you can see the commands, click on the headings. To close the menus so that only the headings appear, click on the background outside the menu. Practice these techniques now.

1. Click on the File heading to pull it down, then on the background to close it up.

Lesson 1/Introducing Windows

2. Click on the Options heading to pull it down, then on the background to close it up.

3. Click on the Window heading to pull it down (see Figure 1-4).

Figure 1-4
Choosing a command from the menu bar

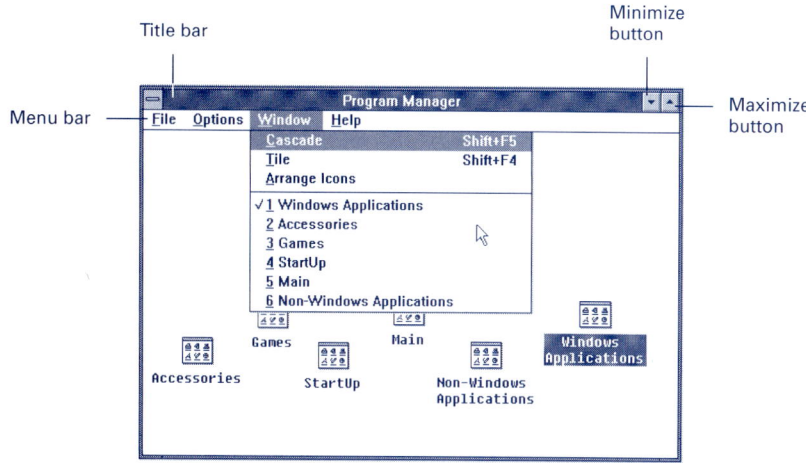

Notice that this menu gives you a list of the program groups. In Figure 1-4, Windows Applications is selected, so it appears on the menu with a check next to it.

4. Click on the background to close it up.

5. Click on the Help heading to pull it down, then on the background to close it up.

You select a command from the menu by clicking on it. You will choose a command from a menu in the next section.

Resizing, Opening, and Closing Windows

You can change the size of any window, making it as small as the icon or as large as the screen. The top line of the window is called the **title bar** (refer to Figure 1-4). At the right corner of the title bar there are two **buttons**. A button in a computer program is designed to resemble a push button you might see on any electronic gadget. When you click on it with the mouse, the button will look as though it has been pressed. The button on the left, with the downward-pointing triangle (▼), is the **Minimize button**. Click on it to display the window as an icon. The one on the right, with the upward-pointing triangle (▲), is the **Maximize button**. Click on it to enlarge the window to cover the entire screen.

Practice changing the size of the Program Manager window by using those buttons.

1. Click on the Minimize button. The window seems to have disappeared! Only a small icon with the title "Program Manager" appears in the lower left corner of the screen. It doesn't appear to have any buttons. How can you expand it again?

2. Click on the Program Manager icon. The Control menu appears (you encountered this menu in an earlier section when you clicked on the program group icons).

3. To restore the Program Manager to its original size, click on Restore. The Program Manager window is again displayed full-size.

4. To expand the Program Manager until it covers the entire screen, click on the Maximize button. The window now covers the screen, and the Maximize button, reasonably enough, has disappeared.

To restore the window to its original size, you could click on the Minimize button, then click on the icon to see the Control menu, then click on Restore. But there is a shortcut: The Maximize button on the title bar has turned into a Restore button (). Click on it to restore the Program Manager window to its original size.

5. Click on the Restore button. The window is restored to its original size.

You can also resize a window manually, by dragging one or more sides until you have the size you want. The technique is to position the mouse on a side or a corner, where the mouse pointer will change from a single-headed arrow to a double-headed arrow (↔) or (↕). Then drag the side until the window is the desired size. Practice changing the size of the Program Manager window.

1. Position the mouse pointer on the right side of the window. *Slowly* adjust it until the pointer changes to a double-headed arrow (↔).

2. Press the left mouse button. A gray outline of the side will appear.

3. Slowly drag the line to the right, then release the mouse button. The window will expand to fill the outline.

Now do the same with the bottom of the window.

1. Position the mouse pointer on the bottom of the window and adjust it until the pointer changes to a double-headed arrow (↕).

2. Press the left mouse button and drag the outline down, then release the mouse button. The window will again expand to fill the outline.

You can also resize a window from the corner.

1. Position the mouse pointer on the right corner of the window until a diagonal double-headed arrow appears.

Lesson 1/Introducing Windows   **11**

2. Press the left mouse button and drag the outline inward until the window is approximately at its original size.

The final techniques you will learn here are opening and closing program group windows. To open a program group window, double-click on it. To close it, click on the **Control menu button** on the left of the title bar (refer to Figure 1-5), then click on Close on the menu. To practice these techniques, open the Windows Applications program group.

NOTE: If you do not have a Windows Applications program group on your desktop, open another program group instead or check with your instructor.

1. Double-click on the Windows Applications program group icon. Your screen should resemble Figure 1-5. The program group in Figure 1-5 contains the program Quattro Pro for Windows; the programs on your computer may differ.

> **CAUTION: If when you double-click the icon, it just moves around the screen, it means you are holding down the mouse button a little too long. Try double-clicking again, holding down the mouse button for the shortest possible time.**

Individual programs are represented by icons, like program groups, but program icons cannot be expanded into windows. You can usually tell program icons from program group icons because the former are much more individual than the latter. This is not surprising, since each software company tries to make its program icon distinctive.

2. Practice shrinking this window back to an icon, maximizing it, and changing its size by dragging the mouse.

Figure 1-5
Double-clicking on a program group icon

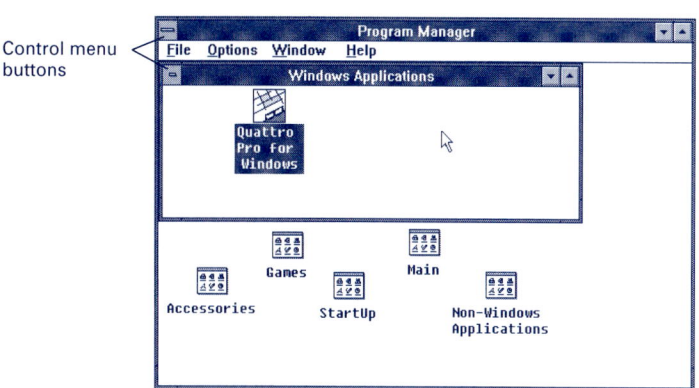

12 First Look at Quattro Pro for Windows

3. To close the window, click on the Control menu button. The Control menu will appear.

4. Click on Close from the Control menu. The window is closed and the program group shrinks back to an icon.

The techniques you have learned for moving the mouse and the icons around the desktop, pulling down and closing up menus, and resizing, opening, and closing windows will work for any windows you use in Windows, as well as for programs designed to run with Windows. Practice these techniques until you feel comfortable working with them.

> **CAUTION:** You can shrink or expand the Program Manager window but do not attempt to close it from the Control menu box! The Program Manager is such an important part of Windows that closing it will exit Windows. If you accidentally try to close it, you will see a box on the screen with the prompt "This will end your Windows session". Click on the button that reads "Cancel" to remain in Windows.

STARTING A PROGRAM

Starting a program with Windows is very easy: Just double-click on the program icon. You must remember, though, to double-click on the program icon, not the icon of the program group. You will practice this by starting the **File Manager** program in order to format a floppy disk, a common computer task. The File Manager is one of several useful programs that comes with Windows. It is generally kept in the Main program group; check with your instructor if you cannot find it after following the instructions below.

1. Open the Main program group by double-clicking on it. The screen should resemble Figure 1-6.

2. Double-click on the File Manager icon. In a few seconds, the File Manager screen appears. The screen should resemble Figure 1-7, but the displayed directories and files will be different.

Note that the File Manager, like the Program Manager, appears in a window, with a menu bar as well as Control menu and the Minimize and Maximize buttons. The left half of the screen shows all the directories on the selected drive; icons for the disk drives appear just above the directories. The selected drive has a box around it. The selected directory is highlighted, and its name appears on the title bar just below the menu bar. All the files in the

Figure 1-6
The Main program group window

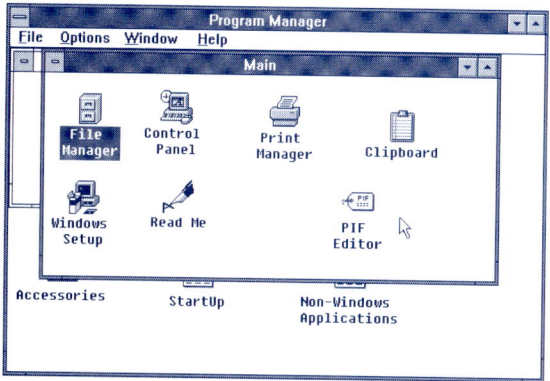

Figure 1-7
The File Manager program

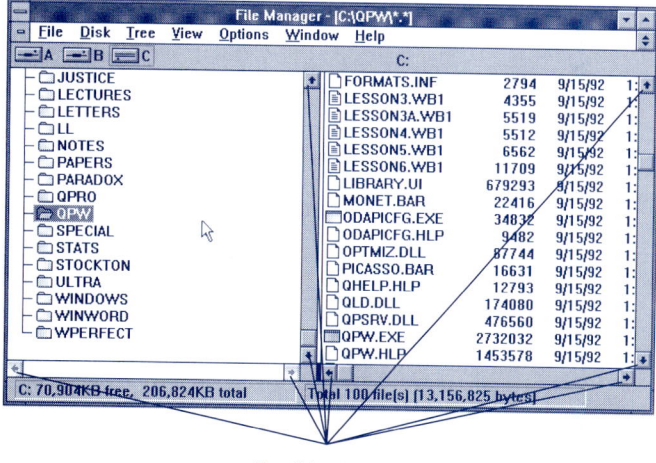

Scroll bar buttons

selected directory are displayed on the right half of the screen. In Figure 1-7, the directory with Quattro Pro for Windows, C:\QPW, is selected, and the right half of the screen shows all the files in that directory. You can select a different drive or a different directory by clicking on it.

Additional features of the File Manager screen are the **scroll bars** that appear at the top and bottom right-hand corners in each half of the screen (refer to Figure 1-7). Scroll bars indicate that there is more to a list than can be displayed on the screen at one time. The bars have upward- and downward-pointing arrows on each end. These are the scroll bar buttons. When you press the scroll bar buttons by positioning the mouse pointer on them and holding down the mouse button, the list will scroll up or down. Scroll bars are found on many Windows programs. Practice using the scroll bars to scroll through the list of directories on the left half of the screen, and through the list of files on the right half of the screen.

14 First Look at Quattro Pro for Windows

1. Press the scroll bar buttons on the left half of the screen to see all the directories on the drive.
2. Press the scroll bar buttons on the right half of the screen to see all the files in the selected directory.

FORMATTING A DISK

You will probably want to save the files you create in the following lessons on a floppy disk. Before using a new disk, you must format it. The command for formatting a disk is on the Disk menu. Select it from the menu bar.

1. Click on the Disk heading on the menu bar.
2. Click on Format Disk. The Format Disk dialog box appears (see Figure 1-8).

Figure 1-8
Formatting a disk in drive A

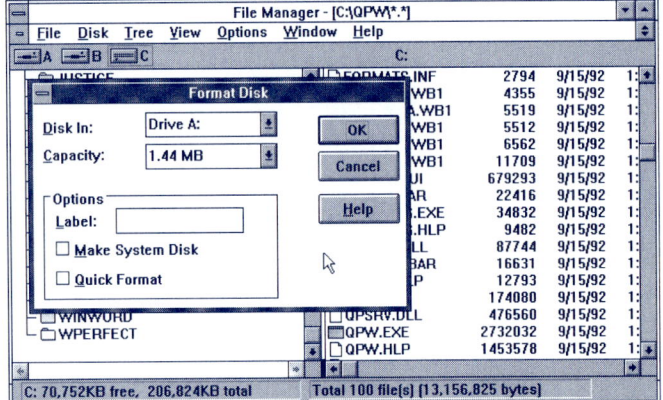

A **dialog box** is a box provided by Windows and other programs when they need more information from you. The simplest form of dialog box will always contain at least one prompt (for example, "Are you sure you want to do this?") and two buttons, with "OK" (or "Continue") and "Cancel". Click on the OK button if you are sure you want to carry out the command or operation; click on the Cancel button if you do not. Many dialog boxes are more complicated and require you to enter information in **edit fields**, which are other boxes that allow you to type information or select from a list of choices. Often one or more of the edit fields will be already filled in because the program has tried to guess what you want to do next. If it has guessed correctly, you need only click on OK. If it has not, you can change the edit fields, then click on OK.

Lesson 1/Introducing Windows   **15**

The Format Disk dialog box requires you to specify two pieces of information: the location of the disk (the "Disk In:" edit field) and the capacity of the disk (the "Capacity" edit field). In Figure 1-8, the dialog box assumes that the disk to be formatted is in drive A and has a capacity of 1.44 MB. To see other options:

1. Click on the arrow to the right of the Disk In: edit field to see the other disks. Click on the arrow again to keep the selection unchanged.

2. Click on the arrow to the right of the Capacity edit field to see other capacities. Click on the arrow again to keep the selection unchanged.

CAUTION: Check with your instructor if you want to change the edit fields.

When the disk drive and capacity are correct:

3. Place the disk to be formatted in the proper drive.

4. Click on OK. A new dialog box will appear with the prompt "Formatting will erase ALL data from your disk. Are you sure that you want to format the disk in drive A?" Your choices are "Yes" and "No".

5. Click on Yes to format the disk. The dialog box will disappear and the disk will be formatted.

EXITING A WINDOWS PROGRAM

To close a Windows program, click on the File heading on the menu bar, then click on Exit. To close File Manager:

1. Click on File on the menu bar.

2. Click on Exit. You will be returned to the Main program group window.

3. Click on the Control menu box, then on Close to close the window.

EXITING WINDOWS

Once you have exited all your Windows programs, you do not need to exit Windows before turning off your computer. Just turn off the switches on the computer and, if necessary, the monitor. But if you would like to exit Windows for some reason, you do so in the same way as you would leave any other Windows program, by clicking on File, then on Exit (see Figure 1-9).

Figure 1-9
Exiting Windows

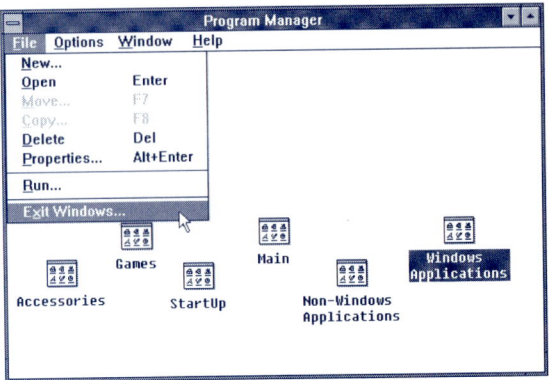

CAUTION: In the course of this lesson you may have rearranged the Windows desktop so that it looks different from when you started. If you want to preserve the changes, click on Options on the menu bar and make sure that there is a check (✓) by "Save Settings on Exit". If there is no check, click on "Save Settings on Exit". Then follow the instructions below to exit Windows. If you do not want to preserve the changes, click on Options and make sure there is no check by "Save Settings on Exit". If there is, click on "Save Settings on Exit". Then follow the instructions below to exit Windows.

1. Click on File on the menu bar.
2. Click on Exit Windows. A dialog box will appear with the prompt "This will end your Windows session". Click on the OK button to exit Windows.

■ SUMMARY OF COMMANDS

Topic or Feature	Command or Reference	Menu	Page
Start Windows	WIN, from C prompt	File ╎ Exit	6
Restore a Window from an Icon		Control menu/ Restore	8
Rearrange Icons	Drag the mouse		8
Select a Menu Item	Click on the menu heading, then on the item		8

Topic or Feature	Command or Reference	Menu	Page
Close a Menu	Click on the menu background		9
Minimize a Window	Minimize button (▼)	Control menu/Minimize	9
Maximize a Window	Maximize button (▲)	Control menu/Maximize	9
Restore a Maximized Window	Restore button (◆)	Control menu/Restore	10
Resize a Window	Drag a window from its side, corner, or bottom with the mouse		10
Open a Program Group	Double-click on the icon	Control menu/Close	11
Close a Program Group			12
Start a Program from Windows	Double-click on the icon	File ¦ Run	12
Scroll a List of Directories or Files	Scroll bars		13
Format a Disk	File Manager	Disk ¦ Format Disk	14
Exit a Windows Program		File ¦ Exit	15
Exit Windows		File ¦ Exit	15

■ REVIEW QUESTIONS

1. What are the standard features of a spreadsheet program?
2. What new features make Quattro Pro for Windows distinctive?
3. What does the keyboard have in common with a typewriter? What makes it different?
4. How does a mouse work?
5. What are the four mouse techniques used in computer programs?
6. Where does Windows get its name?
7. How do you start Windows?

8. When you start Windows, what do you see?
9. What is an icon?
10. What technique do you use to move an icon in Windows?
11. What technique do you use to open a program group in Windows?
12. What technique do you use to start a program from Windows?
13. How do you select an item from a menu? How can you close a menu?
14. How can you change the size of a window?
15. Where will you find the menu item that allows you to format a disk?

■ HANDS-ON EXERCISES

Exercise 1-1 Explore Windows by moving icons and by opening, closing, and resizing windows. Use the techniques you have learned to open each of the program groups and examine their contents.

Exercise 1-2 Each Windows program, including Program Manager, comes with a Help choice on the menu bar. Help provides you with information about the program you are using. It works like a miniature program running inside whatever program you are using: Click on a Help menu item to start the Help program, then click on the Control menu box and select Close to exit it.

Explore Help by selecting Help from the menu bar in Program Manager, then select How to Use Help from the menu. When you have read through the instructions, follow them to learn about Program Manager features. When you are finished, click on the Control menu box and select Close to exit Help.

Exercise 1-3 Windows comes with other useful programs besides File Manager. These include Calculator, Calendar, and Write. They are usually kept in the Accessories program group.

1. Open the Accessories program group and start Calculator. Use Help to learn how to use Calculator, practice by carrying out three calculations, then close it. Start Calendar, use Help to learn how to use the program, practice by entering three appointments, then close it. Start Write, use Help to learn how to use Write, practice by writing a letter, then close it. Note that when closing Calendar and Write, you will be presented with a dialog box asking whether you wish to save your work. Click on No.

2. One of Windows' most important features is that it allows you to keep several programs open at once. Each program appears on the desktop in its own window. The window you are currently working in is called the **active window**, and it is displayed on top of all the others. Windows automatically makes the most recently opened window the active one, but you can make a different window the active window by clicking on it. Explore this feature by opening Calculator, Calendar, and Write so that they are all running at once. You may need to click on the Accessories program group window to get at the program icons. Then, click on each program in turn to make it the active window. You may need to resize windows so that you can see all three programs. To see other ways of arranging the desktop, click on the Window menu, then click on Cascade; next, click on Tile. Finally, close all open programs.

Exploring Quattro Pro for Windows

OBJECTIVES

At the end of this lesson, you will be able to:
- Start Quattro Pro for Windows.
- Recognize the parts of a spreadsheet notebook.
- Move around the spreadsheet notebook.
- Edit cell contents.
- Enter values, labels, and formulas into cells.
- Delete cell contents.
- Use the Bold and Italic buttons on the SpeedBar.
- Select a command from the menu bar.
- Open and close a pull-down menu.
- Save a spreadsheet notebook.
- Close a spreadsheet notebook and display a new, blank spreadsheet notebook.
- Exit Quattro Pro for Windows.

STARTING QUATTRO PRO FOR WINDOWS

Follow these steps to start Quattro Pro for Windows:

1. Turn on the computer and follow the instructions given in the last chapter to start Windows. After a few seconds, the Windows desktop will be displayed.

   The easiest way to start Quattro Pro for Windows is to double-click on its icon (refer to Figure 1-5). The icon may or may not appear automatically, depending on how Windows is set up on your computer. If it does not appear automatically, check with your instructor or try the following:

   a. If the Program Manager appears as an icon in the corner of the screen, double-click on it to display it full-size. If the icon for Quattro Pro for Windows is displayed, skip to step 2.

Lesson 2/Exploring Quattro Pro for Windows   21

b. If the icon for Quattro Pro for Windows is not displayed, double-click on the Windows Applications program group. If the icon for Quattro Pro for Windows is displayed, move on to step 2.

2. Position the mouse so that the pointer is touching the Quattro Pro for Windows icon. It can touch any part of the icon; don't worry if it is not squarely in the middle.

3. Double-click the left mouse button. A small hourglass will appear—the sign that Windows is working. After a few seconds, the logo and copyright notice for Quattro Pro for Windows will appear, and the program will start. The screen should look like Figure 2-1.

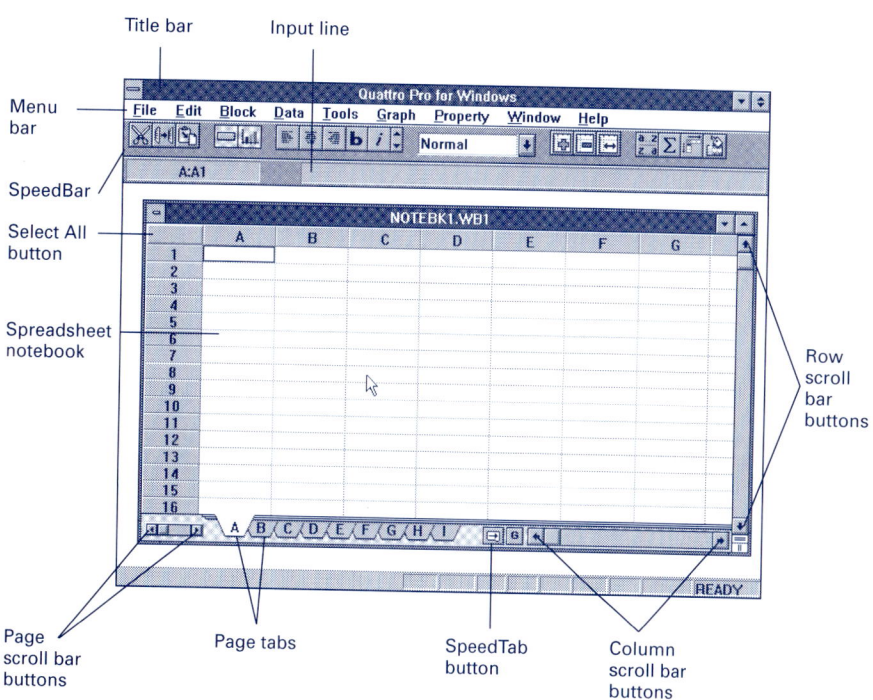

Figure 2-1
Starting Quattro Pro for Windows

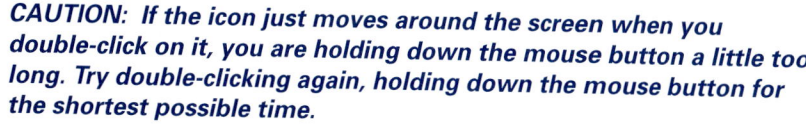

CAUTION: *If the icon just moves around the screen when you double-click on it, you are holding down the mouse button a little too long. Try double-clicking again, holding down the mouse button for the shortest possible time.*

Although the screen may look like one continuous surface, it is actually made up of four parts: the **spreadsheet notebook**, the **SpeedBar**, the **menu bar**, and the **title bar**. When you first start Quattro Pro for Windows, the screen is set up for you to type into a blank spreadsheet notebook. (Initially, the blank notebook is called NOTEBK1.WB1; you can see the name right at the top of the notebook. You will learn how to change the name at the end of this lesson.)

Quattro Pro for Windows begins with this screen because it tries wherever possible to simulate your ordinary working environment. For example, if you were preparing a financial statement by hand rather than on the computer, you would probably start by writing information on a blank sheet of paper. As you work, you reach for tools: a ruler, or a calculator, or scissors and tape. Quattro Pro for Windows assumes, therefore, that you prefer to begin by typing information into the notebook and, when necessary, to reach for various tools accessible from the SpeedBar or menu bar.

THE SPREADSHEET NOTEBOOK

Spreadsheet notebooks are arranged in **pages**, **columns**, and **rows**. The pages are arranged consecutively in alphabetical order: You can see their letters on the **page tabs** at the bottom of the screen. When you start Quattro Pro for Windows, you are automatically positioned on page A. (You will learn how to change the page name in Lesson Eight). Each page can either function as a separate spreadsheet or be linked to other pages. The page that is displayed on top is called the **active page**.

The columns are also arranged consecutively in alphabetical order, beginning with A at the upper left corner. The rows are numbered consecutively, starting with 1 at the upper left corner. Each rectangular intersection of rows and columns is called a **cell**. Each cell has a unique **cell address**, such as A1, D7, H15, based on the column and row it is in.

When you start Quattro Pro for Windows, you are automatically positioned at cell A1. A rectangle, called the **cell selector**, appears at that cell, and A:A1 is displayed in the box just over the left corner of the notebook.

1. Type **My First Notebook**

Notice that the words appear in a line just above the notebook. That line is the **input line**. If you make a mistake while typing, use the arrow keys to move the cursor and the [Del] and [Backspace] keys to make corrections. The cell selector stays at the A1 cell, telling you where the words on the input line will eventually go. At the lower right corner you see the word "LABEL", letting you know that Quattro Pro for Windows assumed you are typing a **label**, a set of alphanumeric characters.

To the left of "My First Notebook", you will also see two buttons, one with an X and the other with a check (✓), as shown in Figure 2-2. These are **buttons** for use with a mouse. If you change your mind while typing, click on the X to cancel the entry. Pressing [Esc] on the keyboard would have the same effect.

Figure 2-2
Entering a label

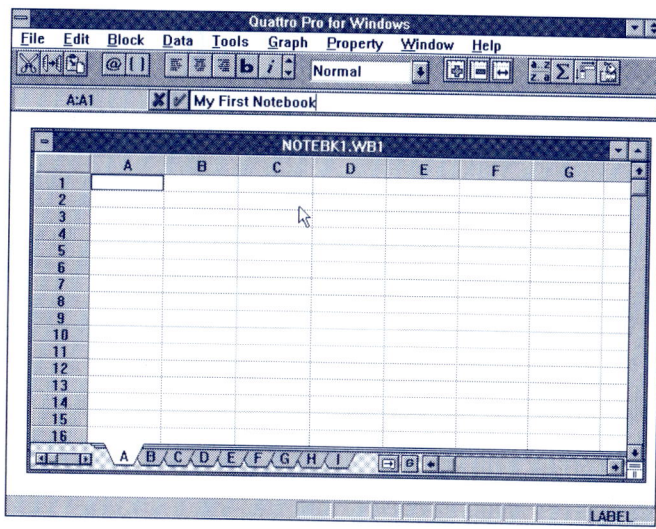

Click on the check button to enter the phrase into the notebook at cell A1; pressing Enter on the keyboard would have the same effect. Since you have been using the keyboard to type the phrase, it is easier to press Enter this time.

2. Press Enter

Now the words appear in the spreadsheet. In the input line, you see "My First Notebook". Quattro Pro for Windows has preceded the words you typed with an apostrophe, which indicates that the words will be a left-justified label. Labels can also be right-justified or centered (you will find out more about that in Lesson Five). The cell selector around cell A1 does not change size, because column A has stayed the same width, even though the label extends beyond it. (You will learn how to change the width of a column in Lesson Three.)

MOVING AROUND THE SPREADSHEET NOTEBOOK

Moving Among Pages

You can move from page to page within a notebook simply by clicking on the page tab. Practice this by carrying out these steps:

1. Move to page B by clicking on the B tab. Page B appears to have been moved in front of page A, letting you know it is now the *active* page. To make sure it really is the active page, type **Page Two** and press Enter.

24 First Look at Quattro Pro for Windows

The box above the notebook to the left says "B:A1", letting you know that you are on page B, in cell A1. The input line says "Page Two". (See Figure 2-3.)

Figure 2-3
Moving among pages

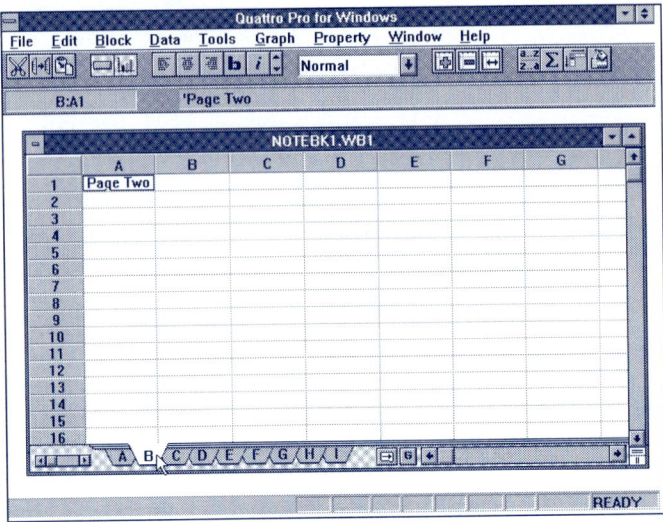

2. Move to page F by clicking on the F tab.

3. Move back to page A by clicking on the A tab.

Each spreadsheet notebook contains 256 spreadsheet pages and a special **Graphs** page, the last page of the notebook (you will learn about graphs in Lesson Seven). To **scroll** through the notebook pages, click on the right- and left-pointing arrows (▶ and ◀) on the **page scroll bar** to the left of the tabs (refer to Figure 2-1). To move quickly to the last page, click the **SpeedTab** button, the right-pointing arrow immediately to the right of the tabs. Once you are on the Graphs page, the arrow will reverse itself and point left. Click on it once more to move quickly to the first page. Practice moving through the notebook.

4. Click on the right-pointing arrow on the page scroll bar to scroll through the notebook.

5. Click on the left-pointing arrow on the page scroll bar to scroll back.

6. Click on the SpeedTab button to move quickly to the Graphs page.

7. Click on the same button (now pointing left) to get back to page A.

Moving Within a Page

You can use the mouse to move within each page by simply clicking on the cell you wish to move to. On page A:

1. Click on C7. The cell selector now appears on C7.
2. Click on G16. The cell selector now appears on G16.
3. Click on A1. The cell selector returns to A1.

On the right side of the notebook is the **row scroll bar**; in the bottom right corner is the **column scroll bar**. Click on the right-pointing arrow on the column scroll bar to display more columns; click on the down arrow on the row scroll bar to display more rows. Click on the left-pointing and up arrows to return.

4. Click on the right arrow on the column scroll bar until columns I through P are displayed.
5. Click on the left arrow on the column scroll bar until columns A through H are displayed again.
6. Click on the down arrow on the row scroll bar until rows 24 through 40 are displayed.
7. Click on the up arrow on the row scroll bar until rows 1 through 17 are displayed again.

You can also use the keyboard to move within each page.

1. The arrow keys will move one cell in the direction indicated by the keys.
2. [Pg Dn] will move one screen down.
3. [Pg Up] will move one screen up.
4. [Ctrl]-[→] (while holding down the [Ctrl] key, press [→]) will move one screen to the right.
5. [Ctrl]-[←] (while holding down the [Ctrl] key, press [←]) will move one screen to the left.
6. [Home] will return the cursor to cell A1 of whatever page is you are on. This is especially useful when a page contains a great deal of information.

The instructions in this book will often tell you to move to a specified cell. You may use either the mouse or keyboard to do so. Take time now to practice moving around the page, so you can see which method you prefer.

EDITING CELL INFORMATION

1. Press [Home] to return to A1 if you are not already there. Once again, you will see "My First Notebook" on the input line.

26 First Look at Quattro Pro for Windows

Suppose you wanted to change the title to "My First Quattro Pro for Windows Notebook". You could retype the whole label and press Enter.

2. Type **My First Quattro Pro for Windows Notebook** and press Enter. The new cell contents will completely erase the old.

There is an easier method for making changes to cell contents than completely retyping them: First make sure the cell is highlighted and then press F2. This will put you in **Edit mode**; you will see the word "EDIT" in the lower right corner of the screen. While in Edit mode, you can use the ordinary typing keys, the arrow keys, and the Backspace and Del keys to edit cell contents. Follow these steps to edit the label:

3. Press F2

4. Edit the label to read "My First Notebook in Quattro Pro for Windows".

5. Press Enter to preserve the changes.

Suppose you've made changes to a cell but decide before you press Enter that you don't like them and want to return to the original contents. You can either press Esc or click on the X in the input line.

> *CAUTION: Pressing* Esc *will only work if you have not yet pressed* Enter. *Once changes are entered, you cannot cancel them by using* Esc. *Use* F2 *to edit them instead.*

ENTERING DATA: LABELS, VALUES, AND FORMULAS

You already learned how to enter labels earlier in the chapter. Quattro Pro for Windows calls any word a label, since that is how words usually function in a spreadsheet.

Entering **values** is just as easy. Quattro Pro for Windows calls a *value* any number or any expression that can represent a number. For example, 5 is a value and so is 5+5.

To see how this works:

1. Move to A3.

2. Type **2**. The input line says "2" and in the lower right corner you see the word "VALUE".

3. Press Enter. A3 now contains the value 2.

A Shortcut for Entering Data

You don't have to press [Enter] every time you enter information. If you press any of the arrow keys to move out of the cell, the information will automatically be entered.

Enter the following values in the following cells, using the arrow keys to enter the information and move around the spreadsheet:

1. Move to A4.
2. Type **2** and press [→]
3. Move to B3. Type **12345** and press [↓]
4. At B4, type **9876** and press [←], then [↓]. You should be at A5.

You can see from what you've entered that numbers are automatically right-justified, so they can be presented in an easy-to-read column.
Formulas are also easy.

5. At A5, type **2+2** and press [Enter]

In the cell, you will see the correct answer, "4". On the input line, you will see what you actually typed, "2+2". The *input line* shows you the "raw version" of cell contents, which includes both what you type and the additional information that Quattro Pro for Windows adds, such as the apostrophe to indicate left-alignment for labels. The *cell* shows you the "processed version"; that is, the calculated formula or the left-aligned label.

Formulas Using Cell Addresses

Formulas don't have to use numbers. Instead, they can use addresses of the cells containing the numbers. After all, why would anyone design a computer program that required you to first type numbers into cells and then retype the numbers into formulas?

1. Move to A6.
2. Type **+A3+A4**. You can use uppercase or lowercase letters in formulas.
3. Press [Enter]

The cell again shows the correct answer—still 4—and the input line shows the formula you used to arrive at that answer. But why, you may ask, do you need that first plus ([+]) sign? Why not just type A3+A4?

4. Type **A3+A4** and press [Enter]

Instead of the calculated number, the cell contains the text "A3+A4". Quattro Pro for Windows has assumed that you wanted to type a label and added the apostrophe to your formula. You can see the apostrophe displayed with the formula on the input line. You need to type a plus (+), or where necessary, a minus (-), at the start of any formula where the first item is not a number. The plus or minus symbol acts as a signal to Quattro Pro for Windows that you are typing a formula not a label. The basic arithmetic symbols you can use in a formula are:

+	plus
-	minus
*	multiplied by
/	divided by
<	less than
>	greater than
=	equal to
<>	not equal to
()	group expressions

In a formula containing several operations, Quattro Pro for Windows multiplies and divides numbers first, then adds and subtracts. For example, in the equation 5+6*17+24, Quattro Pro for Windows first multiplies 6 by 17 and then adds 5 and 24. In the equation A3+A4*B3, Quattro Pro for Windows first multiplies A4 by B3, then adds A3. To change the order of operation, you can group expressions by using parentheses: (5+6)*(17+24) or +(A3+A4)*B3.

Values and formulas can be edited using F2, just like labels.

DELETING CELL CONTENTS

To delete cell contents, position the cell selector on the cell and press Del. To try this:

1. Move to A6 if you are not there already.
2. Press Del and the formula is deleted.

THE SPEEDBAR

The row of mouse buttons above the notebook is called the **SpeedBar**. When clicked, each button carries out a common task. You can find what task a

SpeedBar button performs by positioning the mouse on it. The description of its task will be displayed in the lower left corner of the monitor.

In this book, you will frequently be told to click on SpeedBar buttons. To see how they work, you will change the title "My First Notebook in Quattro Pro for Windows" to boldface, to bold italics, and then back to normal type. You will be using the Bold and the Italic buttons (refer to Figure 2-4).

1. Move to A1.

2. Click on the Bold button. "My First Notebook in Quattro Pro for Windows" will appear in bold type.

3. Click on the Italic button. The label will now appear in bold italics.

To turn off bold and italics and restore the label to its former style:

4. Click on the Bold button, then on the Italic button. The original style is restored.

You can also turn on bold or italics before typing a label, as you can in many word processors.

1. Move to B12.

2. Click on the Italic button.

3. Type **Will this appear in italics?** and press Enter. The label will appear in italics. However, if you move to another cell, italics will turn off.

4. Move to B13. Type **Will this?** and press Enter. The label in cell B13 will not appear in italics.

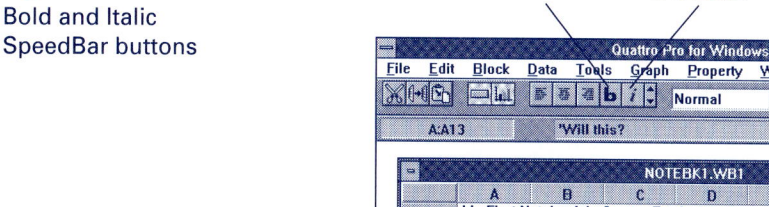

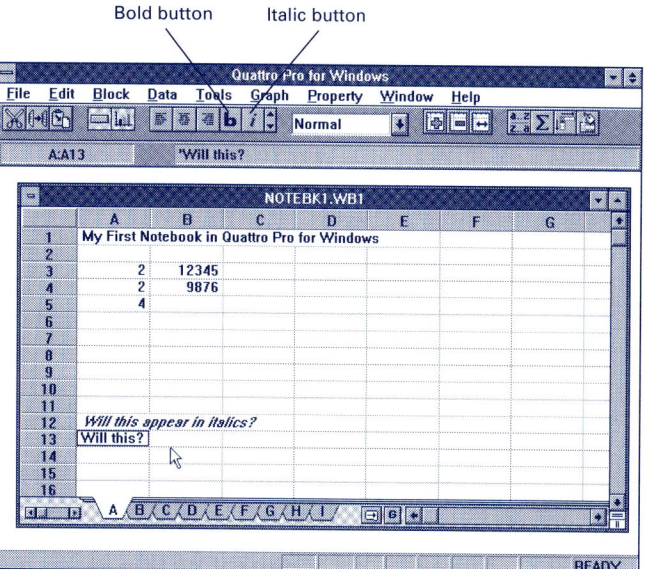

Figure 2-4
Bold and Italic SpeedBar buttons

THE MENU BAR

By now you should be comfortable with the spreadsheet notebook and the SpeedBar. It is time to turn your attention to the menu bar at the top of the screen.

Choosing a Menu Command

The SpeedBar allows you to carry out common tasks, but for many Quattro Pro for Windows operations, you must choose a command from the menu bar. The commands are grouped under the headings you see in Figure 2-5: File, Edit, Block, Data, Tools, Graph, Property, Window, and Help. In order to see the commands, you have to *pull down* the menu under each heading. You can do that in two ways:

1. With a mouse, click on the heading.

2. With the keyboard, press [/] to activate the menu, then press the underlined or highlighted letter for the heading you wish to pull down.

You can move among the different command menus by clicking on each heading or by using the [←] and [→] keys.

1. Try this by clicking on File. As Figure 2-5 shows, clicking on File pulls down the File menu and presents you with a list of commands.

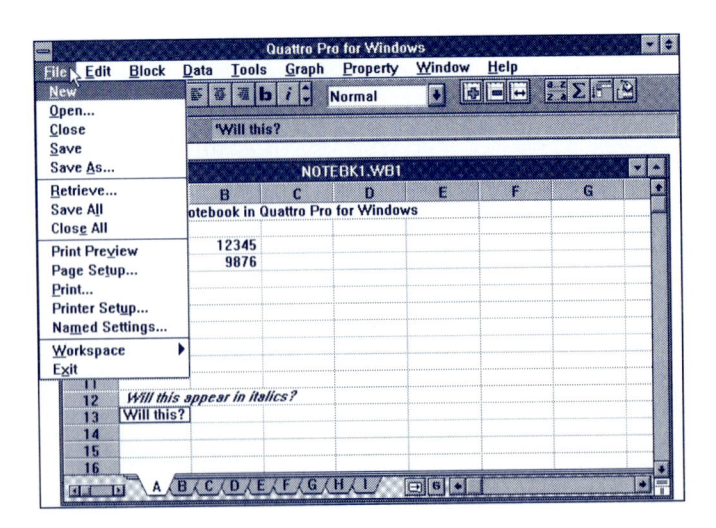

Figure 2-5
Using the menu bar

2. Practice doing this now. Notice that some of the menu items are in light gray rather than black. That is because those commands cannot be carried out at this time: Quattro Pro for Windows tries to save you time by presenting you only with options that you can use. Some of the menu items are followed by a right-pointing arrow (▶); that means that clicking them will reveal an additional menu with additional command choices.

3. To close up a pull-down menu:

    a. With the mouse, click on the background to the menu or outside the menu box.

    b. With the keyboard, press [Esc]

4. To move back to the notebook once menus are closed up:

    a. With the mouse, click on any cell.

    b. With the keyboard, press [Esc]

Menu Terminology

When this book requires you to choose a menu item, you will be told to select Menu bar choice ¦ Submenu choice, which means, "Select the designated menu bar heading, then the designated item from the submenu." You may use either the mouse or the keyboard to select menu items. For example, when this text asks you to select File ¦ Save, you could either:

1. Click first on the File heading on the menu bar, then on Save from the File menu, or

2. Type [/], then **F**, then **S**.

THE TITLE BAR

Above the menu bar is the title bar, which bears the title "Quattro Pro for Windows". This line is your link with Windows: You can think of it as the outer frame of the window holding Quattro Pro for Windows. In the left corner, you can see the familiar Control menu button. Click on it to see a Windows dialog box with the active choices Restore, Minimize, Close, and Switch-To. On the right, you can see the Minimize and Restore buttons.

SAVING YOUR SPREADSHEET NOTEBOOK

> **CAUTION:** Always save your spreadsheet notebook before leaving Quattro Pro for Windows and turning off the computer. Otherwise all your hard work will be lost!

To save your notebook with the name FIRST.WB1:

1. Select File ¦ Save. A dialog box will appear (refer to Figure 2-6).

Quattro Pro for Windows often uses dialog boxes when it requires you to enter information. Many of these contain edit fields for you to enter information. Usually a blinking black line appears in one of the edit fields, indicating that Quattro Pro for Windows expects you to start entering information in that field. To enter data into the field with the blinking line, either type the information, or use the standard editing keys (Backspace, Del, etc.) to edit already existing information. To enter data into another edit field, click on that field with the mouse. The blinking black line will appear in the field. You can also press Tab until the blinking black line appears in the field. Then type in the information. When you have filled in the necessary edit fields, click on the OK button. (You will encounter more dialog boxes in later lessons.)

If the File Save dialog box is set up to save the file in the directory you wish, just type the name you want the file to have and press Enter. Quattro Pro for Windows will automatically add the suffix .WB1. That is, if the dialog box shows disk drive C: and the directory QPW (as in Figure 2-6) and you want to save the file to C:\QPW\, just type the file name. When you press Enter, the file will be saved to the specified disk and directory. If the dialog box shows disk drive A: and you want to save the file to a floppy disk in the A drive, first make sure there is a disk in the drive, then type the file name and press Enter.

The following steps assume you do not want to change the disk drive or directory. When the dialog box is displayed:

2. Type **First**. You can type upper or lowercase (see Figure 2-6).

3. Press Enter.

Your spreadsheet notebook will be saved with the name FIRST.WB1.

If you wish to save the file to a disk drive or directory other than the one displayed, include the disk drive and directory when you type the file name. For example, if the dialog box is set up to save the file to the C:\QPW\ directory (as in Figure 2-6) and you wish to save it to a floppy disk on drive A, follow these steps when the dialog box is displayed:

1. Make sure there is a disk in drive A.

Figure 2-6
Saving a file

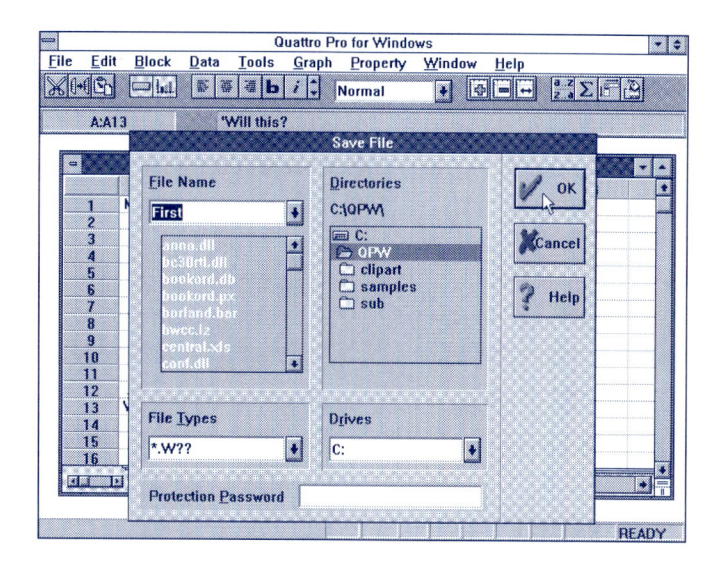

2. Type **A:\First**
3. Press Enter

CLOSING A NOTEBOOK AND DISPLAYING A NEW, BLANK NOTEBOOK

You have finished with your FIRST notebook. If you want to work on another one—or if you want to work on the Hands-On Exercises or move on to Lesson Three—you don't have to leave Quattro Pro for Windows. Instead you can use the Close command on the File menu to close one notebook, then use the New command on the File menu to begin working on another.

1. Select File ¦ Close. FIRST.WB1 will be removed from the screen.
2. If you want to continue working, select File ¦ New. A new, blank notebook will be displayed.
3. Skip to the Hands-On Exercises or the next lesson.

EXITING QUATTRO PRO FOR WINDOWS

To leave Quattro Pro for Windows, select File ¦ Exit from the menu bar. If you have just saved your notebook, this will return you to Windows. If you have not yet saved your notebook, another dialog box will appear, as in Figure 2-7.

Figure 2-7
The screen that appears after you select File Exit without first saving the active file

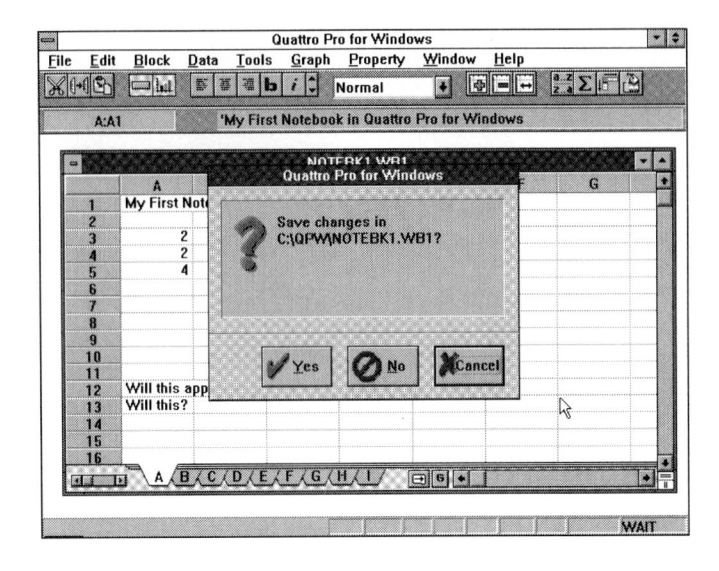

To save your work, click on Yes and follow the earlier instructions for saving your spreadsheet notebook.

1. Select File | Exit.
2. When you see Windows, you can turn off the computer.

■ SUMMARY OF COMMANDS

Topic or Feature	Command or Reference	Menu	Page
Start Quattro Pro for Windows	Double-click on the icon		20
Enter Data in a Cell	[Enter] or arrow keys		22, 27
Make a New Page the Active Page	Click on the page tab		23
Move Among Pages	Page scroll bar		23
Move the Cell Selector	Click on a cell, or use the arrow keys on the keyboard		24
Move Among Columns	Column scroll bar		25
Move Among Rows	Row scroll bar		25
Edit Cell Contents	[F2]		25

Topic or Feature	Command or Reference	Menu	Page
Delete Cell Contents	[Del]	Edit ¦ Clear Contents	28
Boldface	Bold button on the SpeedBar		29
Italics	Italic button on the SpeedBar		29
Choose a Menu Command	Click on the menu bar heading, then on the item		30
Pull Down a Menu	Click on the heading, or press [/], then the highlighted letter in the heading		30
Close a Menu	Click on the background, or press [Esc]		31
Save a Spreadsheet Notebook		File ¦ Save	32
Close a Spreadsheet Notebook		File ¦ Close	33
Display a New, Blank Spreadsheet Notebook		File ¦ New	33
Exit Quattro Pro for Windows		File ¦ Exit	33

■ REVIEW QUESTIONS

1. What are the four parts of the initial Quattro Pro for Windows screen?

2. What name does Quattro Pro for Windows give the initial blank spreadsheet notebook?

3. How are pages designated in a notebook?

4. How are columns designated in a notebook?

5. How are rows designated in a notebook?

6. What is a cell in Quattro Pro for Windows? How does a cell get a cell address?

7. What will clicking on the following do? page scroll bar, row scroll bar, column scroll bar, page tab, Bold button
8. What will pressing the following keys do? [Pg Dn], [Pg Up], [Ctrl]-[→], [Ctrl]-[←], [Home]
9. How do you enter Edit mode in Quattro Pro for Windows? What does Edit mode allow you to do?
10. What is the difference between a label and a value?
11. How do you delete the contents of a cell?
12. What is the SpeedBar?
13. How do you choose a command from the menu bar?
14. How do you close up a menu?
15. How do you save a spreadsheet notebook?
16. How do you close a spreadsheet notebook?
17. How do you exit Quattro Pro for Windows?

■ HANDS-ON EXERCISES

These exercises assume that you run a child-care agency called Nice Nannies Inc. and need to keep track of both clients and nannies. Some clients want full-time child care while others want only part-time help; some nannies want to work full-time while others prefer to work only several days per week. Use the following names, telephone numbers, hours, and wages per hour (for nannies) for both exercises:

CLIENTS			
Mary Tietter	'123-4567	40	
Bill Dejean	'432-8765	24	
Jane Jenkins	'456-7834	40	
Marian Vito	'809-6709	40	
Elaine Petrucci	'987-2365	30	
NANNIES			
Janet Parker	'123-9876	40	$5.00
Tiffany Stevens	'809-4872	40	$6.00
Susan DeMarco	'809-3546	28	$5.50
Debbie DeMarco	'809-3546	40	$5.50
Robert Jones	'456-3859	15	$5.00

Exercise 2-1

Create a notebook using the data for clients and nannies.

1. Enter the label "CLIENTS" in A:A1 and the label "NANNIES" in B:A1. Change them to boldface.

2. Enter the information on clients on page A and the information on nannies on page B. Place each person in a separate row and place each type of information in a separate column. You should enter first and last names in separate columns. You should also type the apostrophe before the number when entering telephone numbers, so that Quattro Pro for Windows knows you are typing a label, not a number. (For example, type **'123-4567**, not simply 123-4567, for Mary Tietter's telephone number.)

3. For each nanny, enter a formula to calculate the weekly salary by multiplying hours by salary. Place the formulas in the column to the right of the salary column.

4. Save the notebook with the name NANNY.WB1.

Exercise 2-2

This exercise builds on the previous one. Each client pays his or her own nanny's salary. Your agency makes money by charging a placement fee of $1500 for full-time child care and $1100 for part-time care. In addition, you charge clients an hourly rate of $1 for every hour of child care.

1. Enter the placement fee for each client and calculate the total placement fees you have collected for these clients.

2. Calculate the amount of money you would earn if all your nannies were working as much as they wanted to. Calculate the amount of money you would earn if all your clients had all the child care they wanted. Should you be looking for more clients to keep your nannies busy or more nannies to satisfy your clients?

LESSON THREE
Creating a Notebook

OBJECTIVES

At the end of this lesson, you will be able to:
- Create a spreadsheet notebook by entering labels, values, and formulas.
- Use the mouse to select a block.
- Use the mouse to copy cell contents.
- Recognize absolute and relative cell addresses.
- Enter cell addresses in formulas.
- Enter absolute cell addresses in formulas.
- Use the SpeedSum button to add up cells.
- Recognize functions.
- Display values in Currency format.
- Use Object Inspector menus.
- Change the width of columns.
- Delete a block.

CREATING A SPREADSHEET NOTEBOOK

As you learned in Lesson Two, you create a notebook by entering information into the blank notebook that appears on-screen when you start Quattro Pro for Windows. To see what you can do with the notebook, imagine that you have been on a number of business trips lately. You have made one trip within the United States, to San Francisco; you have also traveled to Paris and Tokyo. Now you want to document your expenses, either for work or for the Internal Revenue Service. You have kept your receipts, so you could add them up with a calculator. But some receipts are in foreign currency, and you have to change them into U.S. dollars. Besides, wouldn't it be nice to have subtotals for each trip and keep the information in a permanent record that you could print out for your files? Using a spreadsheet notebook would make those tasks much easier.

To find out how, start Quattro Pro for Windows and, when you see the blank notebook, type the title "Travel Expenses" in A1.

1. Type **Travel Expenses** and press [Enter]
2. Move to B3.

You will be entering the information in the chart that follows. The cities go in column B, the type of expenses in column C, the amounts in column D, and the type of currency in column E.

3. Start by entering the information for San Francisco and the label for Paris.

	A	B	C	D	E
3		San Francisco	Hotel	500	
4			Meals	250	
5			Airfare	598	
6			Taxi	75	
7		Paris			

Notice that not all of "San Francisco" is displayed in B3. If you move to B3 and look at the input line, you can see that the label has been entered correctly. But column B is too narrow to display the entire city name. You will learn how to correct that later in the lesson.

4. You could just type in the expenses for Paris and Tokyo. But Quattro Pro for Windows can make things easier for you. You have the same type of expenses for each city, so instead of retyping "Hotel", "Meals", "Airfare", and "Taxi", you can copy the labels you have already typed. There are several ways to copy cell contents. Right now, you will learn how to copy cells by using the mouse to **drag and drop** the cell contents into their new location.

SELECTING A BLOCK WITH THE MOUSE

The first step in copying cells with a mouse is to select a **block**. A block is a group of cells which, when selected, are all acted upon at once by a Quattro Pro for Windows command or feature. A block can be any size, from a single cell (a "group" of one) to all the cells in a large notebook, though some commands can only operate on blocks of certain sizes or types. Blocks are one of the most important features of spreadsheet programs, because they allow you to work with groups of cells at once, rather than requiring you to work with one cell at a time.

In this case, the block of cells you want to copy is C3 through C6, the types of expenses. In spreadsheet commands and formulas, the block consisting of cells C3 through C6 is written C3..C6, where C3 is the starting cell, the two dots (..) make up the **pointer**, and C6 is the ending cell. Drag the mouse to select this block.

1. Position the mouse pointer on cell C3.

2. Press the left mouse button and hold it down while moving the mouse to cell C6. Cells C3 through C6 will be highlighted.

3. At C6, release the left mouse button. The cells will still be highlighted, to let you know that you have selected them. Refer to Figure 3-1.

Figure 3-1
Selecting a block with a mouse

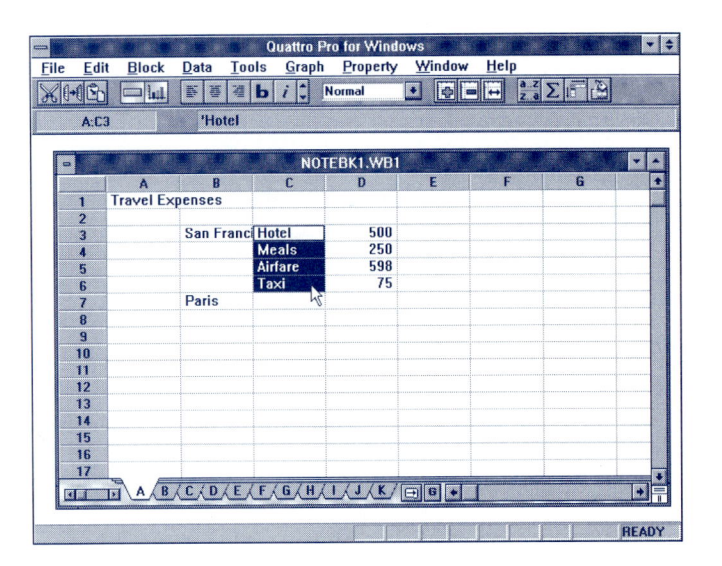

CAUTION: Dragging a mouse precisely where you want it to go can take some practice. If you have highlighted the wrong block of cells, reposition the mouse on cell C3 (the starting cell) and click. The block will disappear. Then try again. To ensure accuracy, you may find it helpful to drag the mouse slowly.

COPYING A BLOCK WITH THE MOUSE

Once the cells are selected, you are ready to copy them to cells C7 through C10 (C7..C10). Since you are copying more than one cell, and since the block forms a rectangle, the easiest way to copy the block is to drag it with a mouse. The basic technique for this is to hold down Ctrl with one hand while using the mouse to drag the block with the other. This is easier than it sounds.

1. With one hand, position the mouse anywhere on the block.
2. Hold down Ctrl with the other hand.
3. Press the left mouse button. The arrow on the block will turn into a small hand, and the outline of the block will be highlighted.
4. Hold down the left mouse button while dragging the block outline until it is positioned to cover cells C7 through C10.
5. Release the left mouse button, then release Ctrl. The block should be copied.

> **CAUTION:** *If you have accidentally copied the block to the wrong place, move to the incorrect cells and press* Del. *This will delete the cells. Then try again.*

Enter the rest of the information for the notebook, as listed in the following chart. Be sure to enter the types of expenses for Tokyo using the drag and drop method of copying cell contents. You have, of course, already entered the labels for Paris; they are included here for reference only.

	B	C	D	E
7	Paris	Hotel	2000	Francs
8		Meals	1570	Francs
9		Airfare	898	
10		Taxi	340	Francs
11	Tokyo	Hotel	51890	Yen
12		Meals	49175	Yen
13		Airfare	1430	
14		Taxi	10835	Yen
15	Total Expenses:			

Be careful to put the labels "Francs" and "Yen" in column E, instead of including them in column D. Column D must have only numbers, so that Quattro Pro for Windows can add them up correctly. The label "Total Expenses:" should be in cell B15. When you are done, return to A1. The spreadsheet should look like Figure 3-2.

Figure 3-2
Travel Expenses data

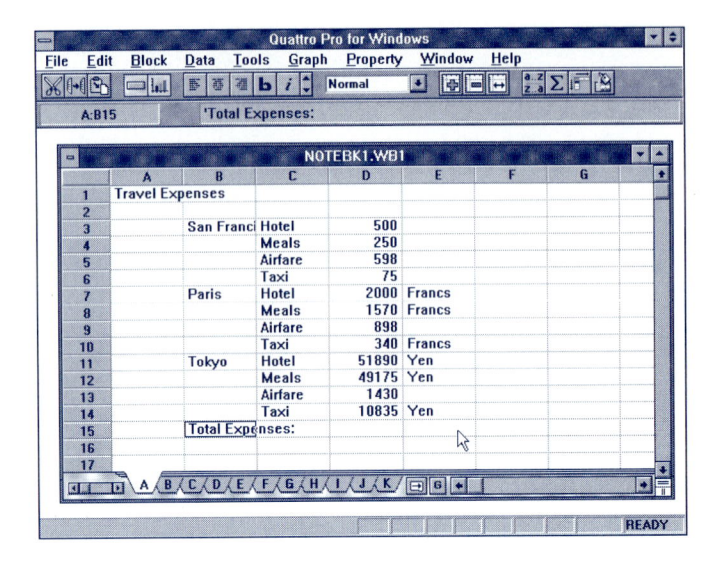

USING FORMULAS

What you would like to do is add the expenses and put the total in cell D15. As the list stands now, though, you can't, because some of the values are in foreign currency.

One way to change that is to use simple formulas. For example, 1 French franc is equal to $.18. You could therefore multiply the value of the francs by .18. Try this for the hotel bill from Paris:

1. Move to D7.

2. Press F2

3. Edit the value to read **2000*.18**.

4. Press Enter

D7 should now say "360". The input line will tell you the formula you used (2000*0.18) to get that result. Since that is in U.S. currency, you no longer need the "Francs" label. Delete it by moving to cell E7 and pressing Del.

> **CAUTION:** Always remember to modify your labels when necessary while working on a notebook. Otherwise you may lose track of what your values refer to.

Using formulas with values will get the correct answer, but it means you have to retype the exchange rate each time. Wouldn't it be easier to just enter the exchange rate once and refer to it whenever you want to use it? Thanks to the formulas you learned about in Lesson Two, that's precisely what you can do.

First set up the exchange rates for francs and yen in a corner of the page.

1. Move to F3.
2. Type **Francs=** and press →
3. Type **.18** and press ↓, then ←
4. Type **Yen=** and press →
5. Type **.0078** and press Enter

Make sure that column F contains the labels and column G contains only numbers.

Now you are ready to edit the formula.

1. Move back to D7.
2. Press F2 to edit the formula and delete *0.18.
3. Press Enter to preserve the change.

> **CAUTION** Whenever you wish to change information you've already entered into a cell, remember to press F2 to edit the cell contents rather than completely erasing them. If you start typing in the cell without pressing F2, you'll lose the existing cell contents. If you notice that you've done this before pressing Enter, you can get the original contents back by pressing Esc.

In the formula, you will insert the cell address G3 in place of .18. Before you type anything, though, we need to explain the difference between relative and absolute cell addresses.

RELATIVE AND ABSOLUTE CELL ADDRESSES

In the last lesson, you learned that you can type in a cell address (G3, for example) instead of a number in a formula. When a cell address in a formula is written G3, it is called a **relative cell address**, because it tells Quattro Pro for Windows to locate the cell by its position *relative* to the formula. In this case, if a formula in cell D11 includes the relative cell address G3, it tells Quattro Pro for Windows to look for the cell three columns to the right and eight rows up.

This is fine as long as you don't plan to reorganize the notebook. But what if you sort the rows into a different order? (We discuss sorting in Lessons Five and Six). The formula in D11 might end up in a different cell, but Quattro Pro for Windows would still expect the formula to refer to a cell three columns to the right and eight rows up. That would result in an incorrect answer.

The way to get around this is to use an **absolute cell address**. You do this by inserting a dollar sign ($) before each part of the cell address, like this: $G$3. That way even if the row containing the formula is sorted, Quattro Pro for Windows will always look in cell G3 for the value to use.

But isn't it a bother to type all those dollar signs? It would be if you had to do it. Fortunately Quattro Pro for Windows provides a shortcut for you, the key F4 . This shortcut is best illustrated by returning to the Travel Expenses notebook. You should be at cell D7.

An Easy Way to Enter Cell Addresses in Formulas

One way to include a cell address in a formula is simply to type it, as you did in the last lesson. But typing is tedious, and you can make mistakes. In many cases, it is easier to simply point to the number you want to use than to type in its cell address. For that reason, Quattro Pro for Windows allows you to point to a number to include it in the formula, by clicking on it with the mouse. Follow these steps to include an absolute cell address in a formula:

1. At D7, press F2 . You will be in Edit mode, and the input line will read "2000".

2. Type *. The input line will read "2000*".

3. Click on G3. The input line will read "2000*G3".

Now you will add dollar signs to the cell address.

4. Press F4 . The input line should now read "2000*$A:$G$3".

5. Press Enter to enter the formula. This calculates the value, 360.

Notice that pressing F4 not only inserts dollar signs in the cell address G3 but also adds the absolute page address $A:. That means that even if you were to move the formula in D11 to another page, it would still refer to the cell G3 on page A.

If you had wished to insert a *relative cell address* in a formula, you would have followed the same steps, except that you would not press F4 . You will use relative cell addresses in Lesson Four.

Follow the same procedure to convert the rest of the values in francs to U.S. dollars. Then edit cells D11, D12, and D14 to achieve the same result for the values in yen. One yen is equal to $.0078, so you must multiply the values in yen by .0078, the value you entered in G4. Once you have converted all the values to U.S. currency, delete the labels "Francs" and "Yen."

When you are done, the values should appear as they do in Figure 3-3.

USING SPEEDSUM TO ADD UP COLUMNS

Now that you have entered your data and converted all the currency to U.S. dollars, you are ready to add up the figures to get your total expenses. You already know one way to add up all the expenses: You could move to D15 and type the formula +D3+D4+D5+D6+D7+D8+D9+D10+D11+D12+D13+D14. That would be a lot of work, though, and Quattro Pro for Windows always tries to save you work. Since adding up lists of numbers is such a common task, Quattro Pro for Windows has provided a special **SpeedSum** button on the SpeedBar to add numbers quickly (refer to Figure 3-3).

You can use SpeedSum to add up any column or row of numbers. The technique is to select the entire column or row you wish to add, *plus* an empty cell just below or to the right of the numbers. Then click on the SpeedSum button. Quattro Pro for Windows will assume you want to add up the column or row and place the result in the empty cell.

Follow these steps to add up the column of numbers in cells D3 through D14 and place the answer in D15:

1. Move to D3.

2. With the mouse, select block D3..D15, using the technique you learned earlier in the lesson (see Figure 3-3).

3. Click on the SpeedSum button. The column of numbers is added and the result, 5327.62, is displayed in D15.

INTRODUCING FUNCTIONS

1. Move to D15 and look at the input line.

The input line reads "@SUM(D3..D14)", which is the formula that Quattro Pro for Windows used to add up the column of cells. The at symbol (@) before SUM tells you that it is a **function**, a built-in formula that comes with the

Figure 3-3
Using SpeedSum

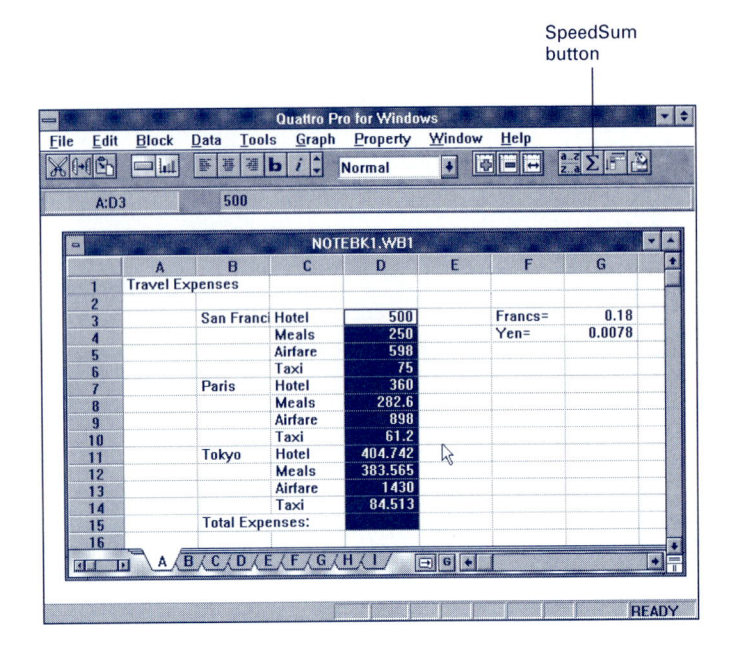

SpeedSum button

[Screenshot of Quattro Pro for Windows showing a Travel Expenses spreadsheet with cell A:D3 containing 500. The spreadsheet lists expenses for San Francisco, Paris, and Tokyo including Hotel, Meals, Airfare, and Taxi. Francs= 0.18 and Yen= 0.0078 are shown in columns F and G.]

program. Quattro Pro for Windows has functions for many common mathematical tasks (you will learn more about them in Lessons Four and Five).

Functions are always preceded by the @ symbol and always include a cell address or cell block in parentheses. In this case, @SUM( ) is the function and D3..D14 is the block to be operated on. Quattro Pro for Windows interprets the formula in cell D15, @SUM(D3..D14), to mean "Add up all the cell contents in cells D3 through D14 inclusive and enter the result in D15."

2. You can see a complete list of all Quattro Pro for Windows functions by pressing [Alt]-[F3] (while holding down [Alt], press [F3]). To move through the list with the mouse, click on the arrows on the scroll bar on the right side. To move through the list with the keyboard, use [↓], [↑], [Pg Dn], and [Pg Up] on the keyboard.

3. When done, click on the X to remove the list from the screen.

CHANGING THE DISPLAY OF VALUES

You now know that your total travel expenses were 5327.62. Wouldn't you prefer, though, to have the figure in currency format? In fact wouldn't the entire column of figures be easier to read if it were in dollars and cents?

What you want to do, in other words, is change the **numeric format** of the numbers. You can modify how numbers appear in a variety of ways, by changing, for example, the number of decimal places that Quattro Pro for Windows displays. The numbers that you entered stay the same, but the way they are displayed on the screen or printed out is changed.

Object Inspector Menus

This time we will convert the values in column D to currency format. For this you will use another of Quattro Pro for Windows' many shortcuts: **Object Inspector menus**. You activate these menus by positioning the mouse and then right-clicking. They are **context-sensitive**: The menu you see displayed in a dialog box or a list depends on what else you are doing in the program at that point. That is, Object Inspector menus automatically sense the tasks you wish to accomplish at a given point and present you with the tools you need for those specific tasks. To help you remember how to call up the Object Inspector menus, Borland has come up with the symbol shown in Figure 3-4. You will see a small version of this picture in the margin of the book every time a new task requiring Object Inspector menus is described.

Figure 3-4
Borland's Object Inspector symbol

Since changing formats and other aspects of the display of cell contents is very common in spreadsheets, Quattro Pro for Windows provides you with precisely the menu you need to modify cell contents. The basic technique is to select the block you wish to modify or format and then right-click to display the menu.

48 First Look at Quattro Pro for Windows

To convert the values in block D3..D15 to Currency format:

1. Select block D3..D15.

2. Right-click anywhere on the block (position the mouse pointer on the block and press the right mouse button). A menu will appear, as shown in Figure 3-5.

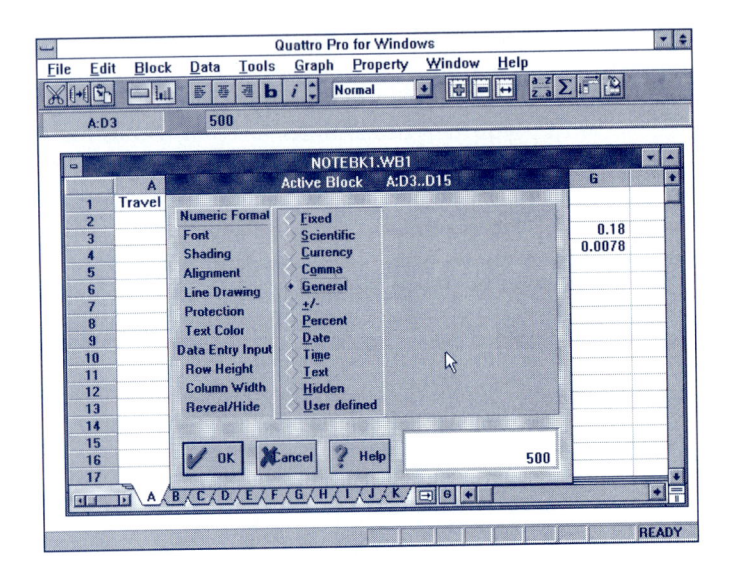

Figure 3-5
Using Object Inspector menus to change the numeric format

The left column of the menu contains a list of **properties**, attributes of the selected block that can be modified. You can select them by clicking on them. The right column consists of possible choices associated with each property. When the menu is initially displayed, the first property, Numeric Format, is automatically selected. The right column therefore displays a list of possible numeric formats.

3. Practice selecting other properties in the left column and note how the right column changes. When done, select Numeric Format again.

4. Since you wish to format the block as currency, select that format by clicking on it in the right column.

5. An edit field will appear, prompting you for the number of decimal places. Quattro Pro for Windows assumes you want two; since that is the usual number for currency, click on the OK button on the menu.

But what has happened to the values for Tokyo Airfare and Total Expenses? All we can see is a row of asterisks! (Refer to Figure 3-6.) Don't worry. Nothing has happened to the values; if you move to D15 and check the input line, you'll see that the function is still entered correctly. The problem is that adding numeric formatting has made the value too wide for the column. To display the value, all you have to do is widen the column.

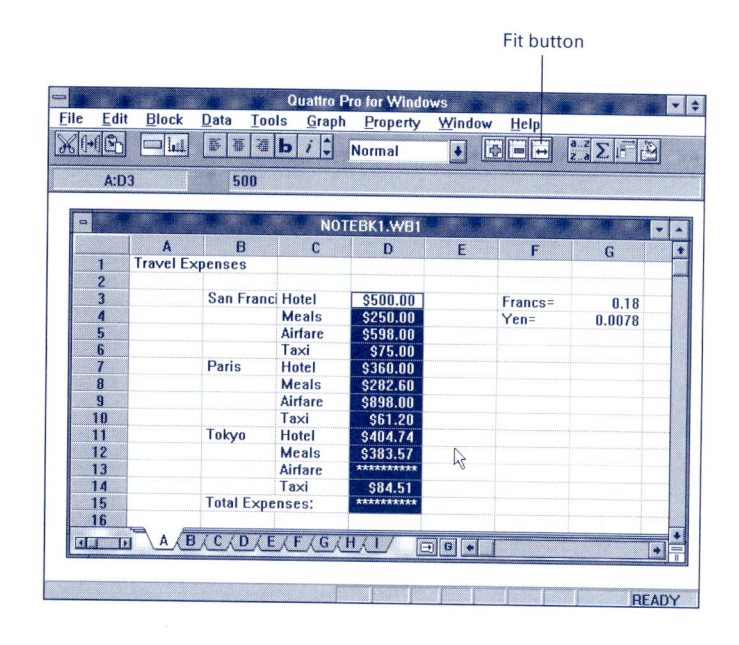

Figure 3-6
Column too narrow for formatted values

NOTE: *Whenever a formatted value is too wide for the existing column, Quattro Pro for Windows displays a row of asterisks in the cell.*

CHANGING COLUMN WIDTH WITH THE SPEEDBAR

The way to fix the problem is to widen the column. There are several different ways to do this. You could use Object Inspector menus; you may have noticed that one of the properties on the menu you just used was Column Width. An easier way for now, though, is to use the Fit button on the SpeedBar (see Figure 3-6). The Fit button will automatically adjust the column width to fit the cell with the longest entry. Use the Fit button on the SpeedBar to do that now.

1. Move to D15 if you are not there already.

2. Click on the Fit button. All of the cells from D3 through D15 should be displayed in Currency format.

Try converting the values in cells G3 and G4 to Currency format on your own. One point to be aware of is that the exchange rate of yen will appear to be 0 if you choose Currency format with only two decimal places. Click on the edit field for decimal places and edit the field to read "4" (or click on the top arrow until the edit field reads "4") and click on OK to properly display the exchange rate for yen.

First Look at Quattro Pro for Windows

The spreadsheet looks much better, but there is still one problem: The label "San Francisco" in B3 is only partially displayed.

Follow these steps to adjust the width of column B so that the entire "San Francisco" label is displayed:

1. Move to B3.

2. Click on the Fit button.

"San Francisco" is now clearly displayed as the column adjusts to fit the longest cell entry. (In this case, the longest entry is actually the "Total Expenses:" label in cell B15.)

When you are done, the notebook should look like Figure 3-7

Figure 3-7
Completed Travel Expenses notebook

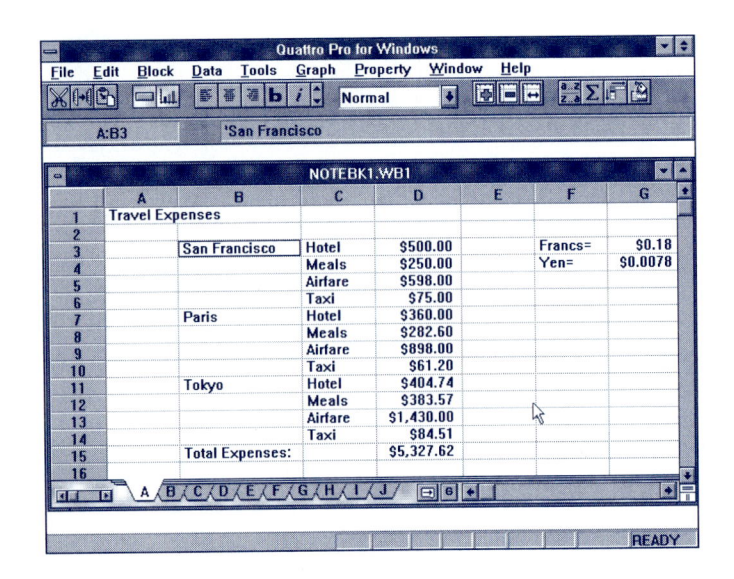

DELETING A BLOCK

You can use techniques you already know to delete a block of cells from the notebook. First select the cells you wish to delete by dragging the mouse. Then press [Del]. The block will be deleted.

> **CAUTION:** Do not do this unless you are completely sure that you want to delete the cells!

Congratulations! You have completed your first spreadsheet notebook. We'll continue to work on this notebook in the next lesson.

Select File | Save, as you learned in the last lesson, to save your notebook with the name EXPENSES.WB1. Then select File | Exit to exit Quattro Pro for Windows.

■ SUMMARY OF COMMANDS

Topic or Feature	Command or Reference	Menu	Page
Select a Block	Move to the first cell in the block, drag the mouse to the last cell in the block		39
Copy a Block	Hold down Ctrl while dragging the block to the new location	Block	Copy	40
Delete a Block	Select the block, Del	Edit	Clear Contents	41
Enter Cell Addresses in Formulas	Click on the cell		44
Enter Absolute Cell Addresses	F4		44
Add a Column of Values	SpeedSum button on the SpeedBar or use @SUM( )		45
Function Menu	Alt - F3 or the @ button on the SpeedBar		46
Object Inspector Menus	Right-click on the cell or block to be modified		47
Currency Format	Right-click on the cell or block to be modified, then click on Numeric Format	Object Inspector Menus	48
Column Width	Fit button from the SpeedBar		49

■ REVIEW QUESTIONS

1. Describe the steps for copying a block of cells using the mouse.
2. You are at A1, with value 5 in B1 and value 6 in C3. Describe the steps for entering a formula that adds the contents of B1 and C3.
3. Explain the difference between an absolute cell address and a relative cell address.
4. Which key inserts dollar signs into an absolute cell address?
5. What steps would you follow to add a column of numbers and put the result in the blank cell immediately below it?
6. Describe the parts of the function @SUM(B1..B6) and explain what it will do.
7. What keys do you press to call up the Function menu?
8. What are Object Inspector menus? How can you display them?
9. What steps would you follow to display cell contents in Currency format?
10. What steps would you follow to automatically adjust the width of a column?
11. How can you delete a group of cells?

■ HANDS-ON EXERCISES

You are the manager of Fine Woolens Ltd., a company that sells selected clothing and household linens imported from Great Britain. You have three stores, in New York, Minneapolis, and Chicago, and you want to create a notebook to keep track of the merchandise in each. For all three exercises, use the following data on store locations, type of merchandise, amount of items, and unit cost in British pounds (£). The data shows your sales for one month.

New York	Sweaters	35	£35
	Capes	25	£50
	Boots, men's	20	£65
	Boots, women's	20	£65
	Tablecloths, small	50	£25
	Tablecloths, large	50	£27

Location	Type	Amount	Unit Cost
Minneapolis	Sweaters	25	£35
	Capes	30	£50
	Boots, men's	50	£65
	Boots, women's	50	£65
	Tablecloths, small	45	£25
	Tablecloths, large	45	£27
Chicago	Sweaters	50	£35
	Capes	20	£50
	Boots, men's	40	£65
	Boots, women's	40	£65
	Tablecloths, small	50	£25
	Tablecloths, large	50	£27

Exercise 3-1

Set up a notebook to keep track of merchandise in all stores.

1. Enter the title of the notebook, "Fine Woolens Ltd.," in A1 in bold type.

2. Enter each store location, type of merchandise, amount, and unit cost in a separate column. Use drag and drop to copy cell contents. Label the columns "Location," "Type," "Amount," and "Unit Cost in Pounds." *Note:* Enter the cost as a number without the pound sterling sign.

3. Use the Fit button to adjust the width of each column.

4. Assume that £1 = $1.67 and enter the exchange rate in a cell. Use a formula with absolute cell references to calculate the cost of each item in U.S. dollars and place the dollar amount in a column to the right of the cost in British pounds. Label the column "Unit Cost in $" and format the column for currency (the decimal places). Widen the column if necessary.

5. Calculate the total cost for all items by multiplying the unit cost in dollars of all items by their respective amounts and place the results in a new column. Display the results in currency format. *Hint:* Use drag and drop to copy the formulas.

6. Use the SpeedSum button to add up the total cost of the merchandise. Display it in Currency format and give the total an appropriate label.

7. Save the notebook as WOOL1.WB1.

Exercise 3-2 This exercise builds on Exercise 3-1. Assume that you sell each item at a 30% markup for clothing and 20% markup for tablecloths. Be sure to include labels for new columns and totals where necessary.

1. Calculate the price for each item and display it in a new column. *Hint:* Enter the markup percentages in a separate block and use absolute cell addresses in your formulas.
2. New York sales tax is 8.25%, Minneapolis sales tax is 5%, and Chicago sales tax is 6%. Calculate the price for each item with sales tax included and display it in a new column.
3. Calculate your total sales for each item, assuming you sell your entire inventory, and place the amount in a separate column.
4. Calculate your total tax for each item, assuming you sell your entire inventory, and place the amount in a separate column.
5. Calculate your total sales and total tax.
6. Use File | Save As to save your notebook as WOOL2.WB1.

Exercise 3-3 This exercise builds on Exercises 3-1 and 3-2. There is no one right answer; be creative and devise the best spreadsheet you can.

You are thinking of opening another store in Southampton, a resort town where many wealthy New Yorkers spend the summer. You would have to rent the store at $5000 per month during the summer season from May through September, but the rent would go down to $3500 per month for the off-season from October through April. You would have to sell most of your merchandise during the summer season to make a profit; however, you expect that the presence of a store in Southampton would act as a form of advertising to boost sales in your New York store. Therefore the store in Southampton might be a good idea even if sales just covered overhead.

1. Assume that the sales data you have entered is a monthly average; you could then estimate yearly sales by multiplying your total sales by 12. Assume that your only costs are the cost of the merchandise plus rent. Add a section to the notebook for the Southampton store showing the inventory you would have to sell to make the store pay for itself. *Hint:* Work out one monthly average for the summer season and another for the off-season.
2. Exchange rates in the European Economic Community have been shaky recently. Keeping sales prices constant, set up a section of the notebook to calculate the difference between total cost of merchandise and total sales if the exchange rate fluctuates by $.20 in either direction. *Hint:* The easiest way to keep sales prices constant is to adjust the markup.
3. Use File | Save As to save the notebook as WOOL3.WB1.

LESSON FOUR: Editing a Notebook

OBJECTIVES

At the end of this lesson, you will be able to:

- Display an existing spreadsheet notebook.
- Change values and recalculate formulas.
- Insert and delete rows and columns.
- Use the Function menu to enter functions.
- Use the Copy, Paste, and Cut SpeedBar buttons.
- Draw lines and boxes.
- Print the active notebook page.

In the last lesson, you learned how to create a simple notebook and how to use labels, values, formulas, and functions to get useful results. In this lesson, you will learn how to modify a notebook to present information more clearly and to get more useful results.

OPENING A NOTEBOOK

The first step is to display your notebook EXPENSES.WB1. The command for this is the Open command on the File menu.

1. Select File | Open. You will see a dialog box with a list of files in the current directory. Refer to Figure 4-1 (the list of files may differ).
2. Click on EXPENSES.WB1.
3. Click on the OK button.

> **CAUTION:** These instructions assume you have saved the file to your current directory. If you saved it to a different directory or disk drive, you will need to specify the directory or drive when you type the name. If you saved the file to a disk in your A drive, follow these steps to display it:
> 1. When the dialog box is displayed, type A:\EXPENSES.WB1 (you can use upper or lowercase).
> 2. Click on the OK button or press [Enter]

Figure 4-1
Opening an existing file

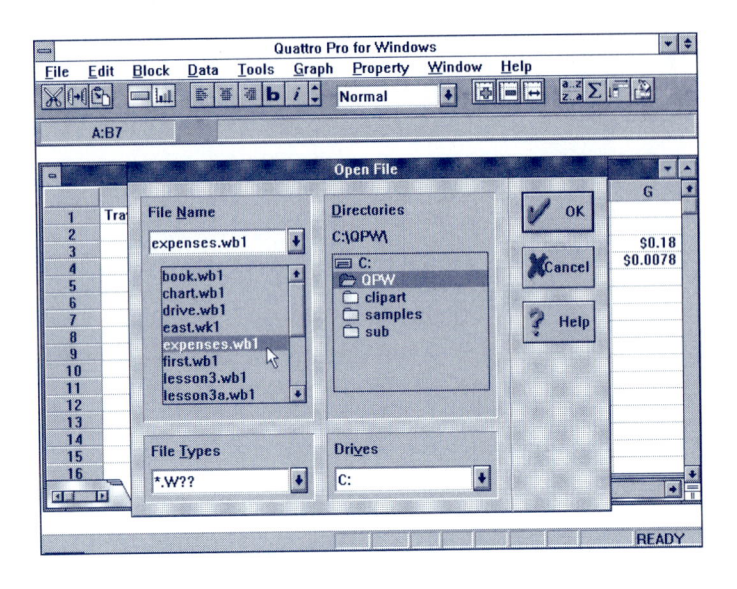

CHANGING VALUES IN A NOTEBOOK

It is extremely easy to change values in a notebook. In fact, notebooks are designed to quickly recalculate formulas with new values. To see how, assume that on reviewing your expenses you find you made a mistake. Instead of spending $500 on your hotel in San Francisco, you spent $516, and instead of $75 for taxis, you spent $78.95.

To make these changes, all you have to do is move to the proper cells and edit the values.

1. Move to D3.

2. Press F2 to enter Edit mode.

3. Change the value to 516 and press Enter.

The notebook will instantly recalculate your total expenses to $5343.62. Notice that the new value, 516, is automatically displayed in Currency format.

Now change the San Francisco taxi expenses to $78.95. Again the notebook will automatically recalculate the total, this time to $5347.57.

You can see an even more dramatic example of the power of notebooks if you try to change values used in formulas. Suppose you discover that the exchange rate you used in calculating the value of francs is wrong. One franc is not worth $.18; instead it is worth $.19.

1. Move to G3.
2. Press [F2], edit the value to read .19, and press [Enter]

Again all the values will quickly be recalculated, with the total expenses now reading $5386.67.

INSERTING AND DELETING ROWS AND COLUMNS

There are other changes you may want to make in the notebook. Suppose, for example, that you would like subtotals for each of the four trips. You already know how to use the @SUM formula to get the amounts. But where should you put the subtotals? Wouldn't it be nice to be able to put them on the line underneath the expenses for each city? In order to do this, you need to add some blank rows beneath each city's expenses. Quattro Pro for Windows allows you to insert rows in a notebook, pushing existing information down to make room for new information.

Inserting Rows

Since inserting rows and columns is such a common spreadsheet activity, Quattro Pro for Windows has a SpeedBar button for it. The technique for using it is to select the row or column that you wish to insert by clicking on the row number button or column letter button, then clicking on the Insert button on the SpeedBar (refer to Figure 4-2). It does not matter if there is information in that row: When you insert a new row, the existing information will be moved down.

This time you would like to add two rows underneath the expenses for San Francisco, one for the subtotal and another to separate it from Paris expenses. That is, you would like to insert two blank rows at rows 7 and 8. To do this:

1. Move the mouse pointer to the button with the row number 7 on it. You may find it easiest to point right at the number 7.
2. Hold down the left mouse button. The entire row will be highlighted.
3. Drag the mouse pointer down until it points at the button with number 8 in row 8, then release it. Both rows 7 and 8 should be highlighted, as a sign that they have been selected.
4. Click on the Insert button on the SpeedBar.

The entire spreadsheet from row 7 will move down two rows. All the information is still in the page, but rows 7 and 8 are blank. The label "Paris", which was at cell B7, is now at cell B9; the rest of the information has likewise moved down, without changing any labels, values, or formulas. Notice that rows 7 and 8 remain highlighted: If you want to change your mind and delete them, they are already selected for you.

5. Insert two rows after Paris and Tokyo expenses. You will need to use the techniques you learned in Lesson Two for moving around the page. When you are done, the top part of the notebook will look like Figure 4-2.

Figure 4-2
Using the Insert and Delete SpeedBar buttons

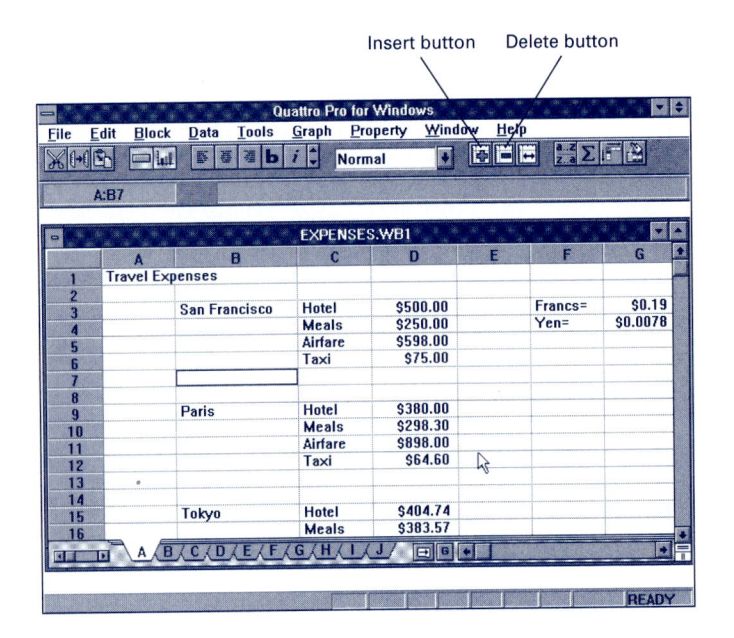

Inserting Columns

You follow the same procedure to insert columns. First select the column or columns where you want to add a blank, then click on the Insert button on the SpeedBar. All the information in that column or columns will be moved to the right.

Try adding two blank columns at columns E and F.

1. Select columns E and F by holding the left mouse button down on the button with the row letter E and dragging it to the button with the row letter F.

2. Click on the Insert button on the SpeedBar.

Look at the screen. No, the information on French and Japanese currency has not disappeared! Quattro Pro for Windows moved it to the right, to columns H and I, to make room for the two blank columns you just inserted. To see it, scroll the notebook until columns H and I appear, then scroll back to the rest of the notebook.

Deleting Rows and Columns

Since you don't need those extra columns now, get rid of them by deleting them. There is a Delete button on the SpeedBar (refer to Figure 4-2) to delete rows and columns, but you should exercise caution in using it.

> *CAUTION: If you delete a row or a column, you delete everything in it. Delete only rows or columns that you are sure you don't want. Unlike some word processors, Quattro Pro for Windows will not ask you whether you are sure you want to delete a section of your work before it makes the deletion.*

The steps for deleting rows and columns are very similar to those for inserting them: First select the rows or columns, then click on the Delete button. You can practice this by deleting the two columns you just inserted, since you don't need them. To delete the two columns:

1. If they are not highlighted, select them by dragging the mouse. If they are highlighted, they are still selected from your last action.
2. Click on the Delete button on the SpeedBar.

The two blank columns will be deleted, and the spreadsheet will go back to its earlier form.

SUBTOTALS: MORE ABOUT FORMULAS

Having used the Insert button to make room for the calculation of subtotals, you can now enter them into the notebook. Since the subtotal consists of the sum of the expenses, you can use SpeedSum to place each subtotal directly underneath the cells containing each city's expenses. The notebook would be easier to read, though, if the subtotals were set off slightly, so why not put them one cell to the right. This involves placing the @SUM function one column to the right of the cells to be added. Since the total will not go directly underneath the cells to be added, we cannot use the SpeedSum button this time. We can, however, either type in the @SUM function or use the Function

60 First Look at Quattro Pro for Windows

menu to select @SUM and use the mouse to select the block, without having to type it out.

To save typing, we will use the latter method. First add a label for the subtotal.

1. Move to B7.

2. Type **San Francisco Expenses:** and press [Enter]

Next begin the formula.

3. Move to E7.

4. Press [Alt]-[F3] to bring up the Function menu.

5. Scroll through the functions, using either the mouse pointer or [Pg Dn] and [↓], until you reach SUM.

6. Select SUM by clicking on it. Then click on the OK button. The input line will read "@SUM(".

Then select the block of cells to add.

1. Move to D3.

2. Drag the mouse button to extend the block through D6. The input line will read "@SUM(D3..D6".

3. Type **)** to end the function.

4. Press [Enter] to calculate the subtotal, 1442.95.

Finally use Object Inspector menus (discussed in Lesson Three) to change Numeric format of the cell to Currency.

1. Right-click on E7.

2. Select Numeric Format, Currency, 2 decimal places.

3. Click on the OK button. Once again you will see a row of asterisks. You know what to do about them.

4. Click on the Fit button to widen the column. Cell E7 should now show the correct value, $1442.95.

COPYING CELL CONTENTS

You could now repeat the entire procedure for each of the cities. Once again though, Quattro Pro for Windows can save you time and energy by allowing you to copy cells to get the subtotals for Paris and Tokyo expenses.

You already know how to do this using the mouse to drag and drop. But drag and drop only lets you make one copy at a time. A more efficient way to copy in this case is to use the **Copy** and **Paste** buttons on the SpeedBar (refer to Figure 4-3). The procedure is to select the cells you wish to copy and click on the Copy button. Then select the cells you wish to copy to and click on the Paste button.

Copying and Modifying Labels

Try this first with the subtotal labels. Since the label you would use for the Paris subtotal, "Paris Expenses:", is very similar to the label you already have, "San Francisco Expenses:", you can save typing by copying and editing the label.

1. Move to B7, the cell with "San Francisco Expenses:".
2. Click on the Copy button on the SpeedBar.
3. Move to the first cell you wish to copy the information to, cell B13.
4. Click on the Paste button. The label will be copied to B13.
5. Press [F2]. Edit the label to read "Paris Expenses:" and press [Enter]
6. Move to the next cell you wish to copy the information to, cell B19. Click on the Paste button. Then press [F2]. Edit the label to read "Tokyo Expenses:" and press [Enter] (refer to Figure 4-3).

Copying Numbers

Use precisely the same procedure to copy numbers. When you copy a cell with numbers, you also copy all the formats that go along with that cell.

Copying Formulas and Functions

Copying formulas and functions with cell addresses is a little more complicated. If a formula contains an absolute cell address, it will continue to refer to that cell address even if copied to another part of the notebook. But if a formula contains a relative cell address, the formula will always refer to whatever cell is in the same relative position. For example, if a formula referring to a cell three columns to the right and eight rows up is copied to a new position, it will continue to refer to whatever cell is three columns to the right and eight rows up from its new position.

Take a look at the formula in cell E7 by moving to E7 and looking at the input line. The formula uses relative cell addresses. If you wish to copy it to get subtotals for the other cities, you must copy it to a cell with the same position relative to the cells you wish to add. Fortunately that is precisely what you wish to do.

It is easy to demonstrate why. Using the same procedure you used to copy labels, copy the formula in cell E7 to E13.

1. Move to E7, then click on the Copy button.

2. Move to E13, then click on the Paste button.

The notebook will calculate Paris expenses as $1640.90. Look at the formula on the input line. You will see that the formula has been automatically changed to point to cells D9..D12. You can also see that all formatting has been copied with the formula.

What would happen if you did not position the new formula correctly? Try it by copying the formula in E13 to D13, using the same procedure you just learned. The result in D13 will be $0.00; if you move to D13 and look at the formula on the input line, you will see why. The cell addresses in the formula have been automatically changed to retain the same position relative to the formula itself: They now refer to cells C9..C12. Since those cells don't contain any values, their sum is 0.

Press [Del] to delete the formula, since you have no need for an incorrect formula in the notebook.

Copy the formula to E19 by moving to E19 and clicking on the Paste button. This will give you the subtotal for Tokyo expenses. When you are done, the bottom part of the notebook should look like Figure 4-3.

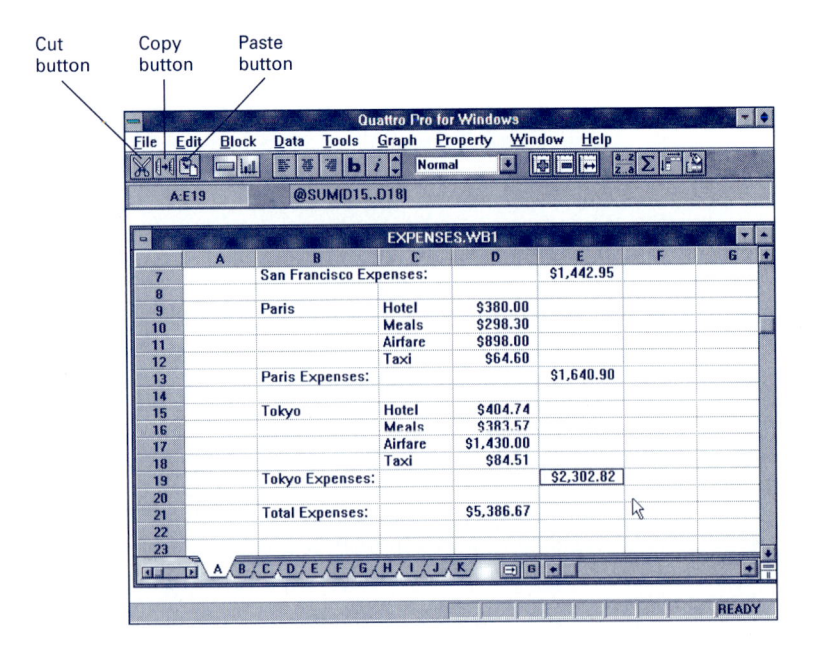

Figure 4-3
Using the Cut, Copy, and Paste SpeedBar buttons

MOVING CELL CONTENTS

You have now found subtotals for the expenses in each city. In the process, the notebook has become a little unbalanced, since the value for Total Expenses is still located in the column with individual expenses at D21, not under the subtotals in column E.

That can easily be changed by moving the cell contents. To move a block (rather than copy it), use the **Cut** button on the SpeedBar (see Figure 4-3) together with the Paste button.

1. Move to D21.

2. Click on the Cut button. The cell contents will apparently disappear.

3. Move to E21 and click on the Paste button. The cell will display the value for Total Expenses, "$5,386.67". (If you wished to make several copies of the cell contents, you could Paste them in several cells.)

If you look at the input line while at E21, you can see that this time Quattro Pro for Windows did not change the cell addresses in the formula. Since you used the Cut rather than the Copy button, Quattro Pro for Windows assumed you wanted the formula to refer to the original cell addresses.

DRAWING LINES AND BOXES

The next editing technique does not help with calculation, but it makes spreadsheets easier to read. This technique involves drawing lines and boxes to clarify or enhance the presentation of data. This feature can make the difference between a spreadsheet that looks like a rough draft and one that looks like a final, polished copy. It is especially useful when designing spreadsheets that your boss or clients will see. Remember when drawing lines and boxes, though, that a little spreadsheet enhancement goes a long way. Too many lines and boxes will make it harder, not easier, to understand your data.

For this example, you will draw only single lines under the expenses of each subgroup and a single-line box around each subtotal. The procedure is to select the block of cells you want to underline or place in a box and right-click to bring up the Object Inspector menu.

1. Move to C6, the last of the San Francisco expenses.

2. Select block C6..D6 by dragging the mouse.

3. Right-click on the block. The Object Inspector menu will appear.

4. Select Line Drawing from the left-hand column to display the menu shown in Figure 4-4.

Figure 4-4
Using Object Inspector menus to draw lines and boxes

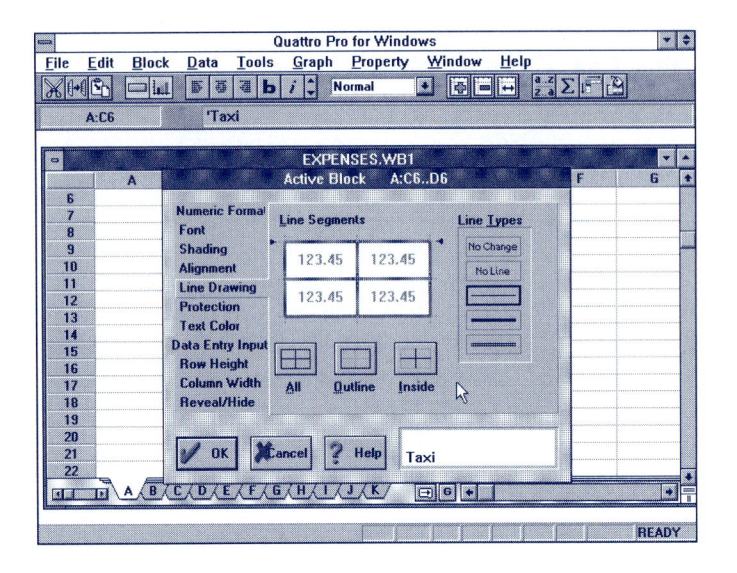

Take a few moments to examine the menu. The Line Types column on the right displays the types of lines you can draw. The bottom three buttons allow you to choose either single lines, thick single lines, or double lines. The first button, with the words "No Change", allows you to change your mind after altering existing lines and boxes and return to your initial selection. The second button, "No Line", allows you to remove existing lines and boxes. Just to the left, under Line Segments, you will see a box divided into four parts. This allows you to choose the position of the line. Click on the top of the box to place a line above the block you selected; click on the sides to place a line on the sides of the block; click on the bottom to place a line underneath a block. The three boxes below these four allow you to position the lines around or between cells in the block.

To draw a line underneath the block you have selected:

1. Click on the button for thick single lines (refer to Figure 4-4).

2. Click on the bottom of the Line Segments box.

3. Click on the OK button on the menu. You will be returned to the notebook. Move the cell selector. As you can see, you have drawn a line under the San Francisco expenses.

To draw a single-line box around the San Francisco subtotal:

1. Move to E7.

2. Right-click to bring up the Object Inspector menu and select Line Drawing.

3. Click on the button for thick single lines.

4. Click on the Outline button to draw a box.

5. Click on the OK button on the menu. You will be returned to the notebook. If you move the cell selector, you will see that you have drawn a box around the San Francisco subtotal.

6. Follow the same procedure to draw lines underneath the rows with Paris expenses (C12..D12) and Tokyo expenses (C18..D18) and to draw boxes around the Paris and Tokyo subtotals (E13 and E19).

As a final enhancement to the notebook, you will change the title "Travel Expenses" and the last line of the notebook to bold type. In Lesson Two you learned how to change a single cell to bold: Select the cell and click on the Bold button on the SpeedBar. You can modify a block of cells in the same way, by first selecting it, then clicking the Bold button.

First change the title.

1. Move to A1.

2. Click on the Bold button on the SpeedBar. "Travel Expenses" is changed to bold type.

Next change the last line of the notebook, containing the information for total expenses.

1. Move to B21 ("Total Expenses") and select the block B21..E21.

2. Click on the Bold button on the SpeedBar. "Total Expenses" has been changed to bold type.

PRINTING THE ACTIVE NOTEBOOK PAGE

> **CAUTION:** This section should only be tried if Windows has been set up for a printer, the computer is connected to the printer, and the printer is turned on.

Often the only way to properly examine a notebook is to print it out. Quattro Pro for Windows makes it easy for you to print out a quick copy of your notebook page (in Lesson Nine you will learn more advanced printing techniques).

The Print command is on the File menu. In order for the Print command to work, the block you wish to print must be specified. You can do this by using the mouse and selecting the block, but right now you don't have to: The first time you print a notebook, Quattro Pro for Windows assumes you want to print all the information on the active page. Since that is what you want to do, printing is very simple.

66 First Look at Quattro Pro for Windows

1. Select File ¦ Print.
2. The Print menu appears (see Figure 4-5). The Print block edit field shows that Quattro Pro for Windows has already selected the block comprising all the information on the page (A1..G21). *Note:* The printer in your Print menu may be different.

Figure 4-5
Printing the active page

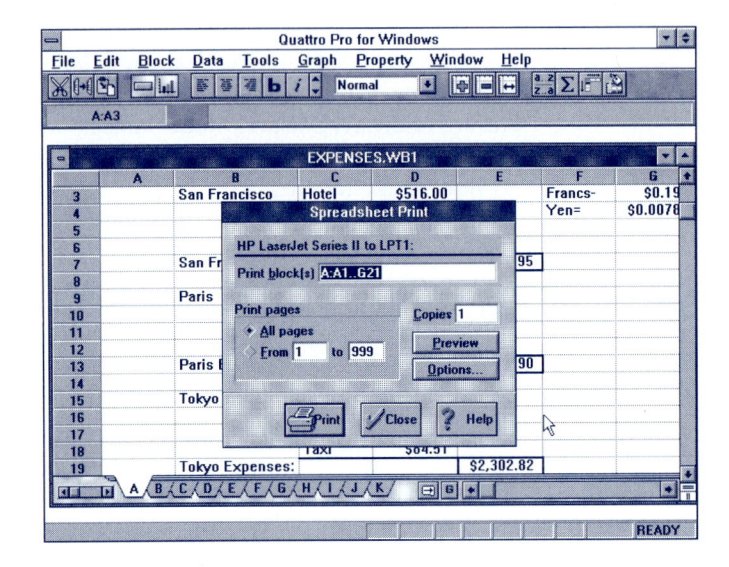

3. Click the Print button. In a few minutes, the notebook page will be printed.

You have now learned basic notebook editing skills. Save EXPENSES.WB1, then leave Quattro Pro for Windows by selecting File ¦ Exit.

■ SUMMARY OF COMMANDS

Topic or Feature	Command or Reference	Menu	Page
Open an Existing Notebook	Click on the file from the list, then click on OK	File ¦ Open	55
Select a Row	Click on the row number button		57
Select a Column	Click on the column letter button		58

Lesson 4/Editing a Notebook **67**

Topic or Feature	Command or Reference	Menu	Page
Insert a Row	Insert button on the SpeedBar	Block ǀ Insert ǀ Row	57
Insert a Column	Insert button on the SpeedBar	Block ǀ Insert ǀ Column	58
Delete a Row	Delete button on the SpeedBar	Block ǀ Delete ǀ Row	59
Delete a Column	Delete button on the SpeedBar	Block ǀ Delete ǀ Column	59
Copy a Block	Copy and Paste buttons on the SpeedBar	Block ǀ Copy	60
Move a Block	Cut and Paste buttons on the SpeedBar	Block ǀ Move	63
Draw Lines and Boxes	Right-click on the cell or block to be modified, then click on Line Drawing	Object Inspector menus	63
Print the Active Page		File ǀ Print	65

■ REVIEW QUESTIONS

1. Identify and briefly describe the functions of the following SpeedBar buttons:

2. How do you open a notebook? What is the difference between opening a notebook and creating a notebook?

3. How do you select a row? A column?

4. When Quattro Pro for Windows inserts blank rows, do the new rows appear above or below the selected row?

5. When Quattro Pro for Windows inserts blank columns, do the new columns appear to the left or to the right of the selected column?

6. Cell C1 contains the formula +B4*K16. If you use the Copy and Paste buttons to copy it to C5, will the new formula in C5 be different? If so, what will it be?

7. Cell C1 contains the formula +$B$4*$K$16. If you use the Copy and Paste buttons to copy it to C5, will the new formula in C5 be different? If so, what will it be?

8. Cell C1 contains the formula +D17-D16. If you use the Cut and Paste buttons to move it to C5, will the new formula in C5 be different? If so, what will it be?

9. What steps would you follow to place a double line underneath cells E5..G5?

10. Describe the procedure for printing the active page of a notebook.

11. To print a notebook that contains information on page A in cells A1..C15, what must the Print block edit field on the Print menu be set for?

■ HANDS-ON EXERCISES

These exercises build on the notebooks you created in the previous lesson. If you completed Exercise 3-1 only, open WOOL1.WB1; if you completed Exercises 3-1 and 3-2, open WOOL2.WB1; if you completed Exercises 3-1, 3-2, and 3-3, open WOOL3.WB1.

If you completed Exercise 3-1 only: Assume that you sell each item at a 30% markup for clothing and a 20% markup for tablecloths.

a. Calculate the price for each item and display it in a new column. *Hint:* Enter the markup percentages in a separate block and use absolute cell addresses in your formulas.

b. Calculate your total sales for each item, assuming you sell your entire inventory, and place the amounts in a separate column. Then calculate your total sales.

Exercise 4-1 Edit the notebook in the following ways:

1. Calculate subtotals for each store for total cost and total sales. Insert lines and edit labels as necessary. Move the cells with total cost and sales for all stores so that they are lined up with the subtotals.

2. Place a double line underneath the title, single lines under the column headings, single-line boxes around subtotals, and double-line boxes around the totals for all stores. Widen columns as necessary.

3. Print the notebook.

4. Save the notebook with the changes.

Exercise 4-2

Quattro Pro for Windows has a SpeedFormat button on the SpeedBar that gives you predesigned formats. Consult the Command Summary at the back of the book to identify the SpeedFormat button. It is a quick way to produce presentation-quality notebooks without designing them yourself. The procedure is to select the block you want to format, click on the SpeedFormat button, then double-click on the format you prefer.

1. Select a block containing the information for each store in turn and use SpeedFormat to format it. Choose whichever format you prefer; it is recommended that you use the same format for each store. *Note:* If you are using WOOL3.WB1, format the information for New York, Minneapolis, and Chicago only.

2. Print the information for the New York, Minneapolis, and Chicago stores. If you are using WOOL2.WB1, Quattro Pro for Windows will specify the correct block automatically. If you are using WOOL3.WB1, you will have to enter the correct block in the Print block edit field.

3. Save the notebook with the changes.

Exercise 4-3

This exercise assumes you have completed Exercise 3-3 in the previous lesson and are using WOOL3.WB1. There is no one right answer; be creative and devise the best spreadsheet you can.

You have decided that it makes no sense to open a store in Southampton, because it is a beach resort and it is unlikely that you could sell enough woolen goods in the summer to make it pay. Instead you are investigating opening a store in Stowe, Vermont. Stowe's high seasons are from September through November for fall foliage and from January through March for skiing; it gets many visitors even during the off-season, from April through August. Rents are $5000 during January and February and $3000 during all other months. You expect to sell 40% of yearly sales from September through December, as visitors buy presents for Christmas. The other 60% should be spread out over the year.

1. Use Cut and Paste to move the information on the Southampton store to page B of the notebook. Then edit the labels to fit a new store in Stowe.

2. Quattro Pro for Windows has a SpeedFill button on the SpeedBar that automatically enters items in a series. You can use it to enter all the months in a year. Enter **January** in cell B3. Then select the block B3..B14 and click on SpeedFill. The names of the months will be entered. Use this feature to develop a spreadsheet to estimate what your monthly sales should be to make the new store break even (total yearly sales = total yearly costs plus rent). *Hint:* Use absolute cell addresses to enter the rents for each month.

3. You cannot expect this store to boost sales in the New York store, so you would like to make a profit. What should your monthly sales be to clear a profit equal to 10% of your costs?

4. Save the notebook with the changes.

LESSON FIVE: More Editing, More Functions

OBJECTIVES

At the end of this lesson, you will be able to:

- Specify column width using Object Inspector menus.
- Use the keyboard to select a block [Shift]-[F7].
- Change the alignment of cell contents.
- Use the SpeedSort button on the SpeedBar.
- Use the @COUNT, @MAX, and @MIN functions.
- Use the @PMT function to calculate payments on a loan.
- Create links between different sections of a spreadsheet notebook.
- Use the @IF function to test for certain conditions.

In this lesson, you will use some of Quattro Pro for Windows' decision-making techniques. Since Quattro Pro for Windows can recalculate formulas so quickly, you can use its built-in functions together with its editing and copying techniques to "plug in" a range of different values to the same formula. This lesson will also introduce a few more techniques for enhancing the appearance of a spreadsheet.

For this lesson, imagine that you are in the market for a vacation home. You need a loan to pay for it and you want to calculate the monthly payments to make sure you can afford them. The first step is to create a spreadsheet showing the list of properties you are considering. The completed spreadsheet is shown in Figure 5-1. Follow these steps to create it:

1. To enter the title, make sure [Caps Lock] is on and move to B1.

2. Type **VACATION PARADISE** and press [Enter]

3. To enter the column headings, move to A3.

4. Type **LOCATION** and press [→]

5. Type **DESCRIPTION** and press [→]

6. Type **PRICE** and press [Enter]

7. Press [Caps Lock] again to turn it off.

SPECIFYING COLUMN WIDTH

The labels you have entered don't look very attractive. The label "PRICE" overlaps the label "DESCRIPTION", making it hard to read. Although you know how to use the Fit button on the SpeedBar to change the width of columns, if you used it this time, you would have to recalculate the column width each time you added a longer entry. Wouldn't it be easier to simply specify a width in advance?

Because specifying column width when starting a spreadsheet makes it easier to read the labels and values as you enter them, Quattro Pro for Windows provides a way to do so: You can use the Object Inspector menu to change column width. The procedure for activating the Column Width feature is similar to that for specifying Numeric Format or Line Drawing. Right-click on the column or any cell in it. Then select Column Width and type the width. When you start Quattro Pro for Windows, the default column width is 9 characters.

You will change the width of column A in this notebook to 20, column B to 35, and column C to 15. Start with column A.

1. Right-click on column A. The Object Inspector menu will show you a list of modifications.

2. Select Column Width.

3. Type **20** and press [Enter]

Now move on to columns B and C.

1. Right-click on column B. The Object Inspector menu will show you a list of modifications.

2. Select Column Width.

3. Type **35** and press [Enter]

4. Right-click on column C.

5. Select Column Width.

6. Type **15** and press [Enter]

You have now increased the widths of all three columns to accommodate the data you will enter.

The next step is to add a double line under the column headings. You already know the procedure for this: Select the cells (in this case, A3..C3), right-click to bring up the Object Inspector menu, and select Line Drawing. You can use the mouse to select the cell block, as you did in the preceding chapters. But Quattro Pro for Windows allows you to use the keyboard to select blocks as well, and you will find it helpful to know both techniques.

USING THE KEYBOARD TO SELECT A BLOCK

To use the keyboard to select a block, move to the first cell in the block and press Shift-F7 (while holding down Shift, press F7). This is called **Extended mode;** you will see the letters EXT in the lower right corner of the screen. Then use the arrow keys and Pg Up and Pg Dn to extend the block to all the cells you wish to include. You can use Shift-F7 with any command that requires you to specify a block. To unselect the block and leave Extended mode, press Esc.

To practice this technique, draw a double line under cells A3..C3.

1. Move to A3 and press Shift-F7. Use → to extend the block to C3.

2. Right-click on the block.

3. Select Line Drawing and specify a double line under the cell block (refer to Lesson Four if you need help).

4. Click on the OK button. Quattro Pro for Windows has placed a double line under the column headings.

NOTE: *In future exercises, you may use either the mouse or* Shift-F7 *when instructed to select a cell block.*

Now you are ready to enter the notebook data. Move to A5 and enter the information in the following chart in cells A5 through C18.

> **CAUTION: Some of the descriptions begin with numbers. For that reason, you must first type an apostrophe (') to let Quattro Pro for Windows know you are typing a label, not a number. The apostrophe will not appear in the cell, but it will appear on the input line when the cell is highlighted.**

	A	B	C
5	NEW YORK CITY	PENTHOUSE WITH GARDEN	695000
6	NEW YORK CITY	'37 ROOM MANSION	7750000
7	NEW YORK STATE	'18 ACRE ISLAND WITH MANSION	1199000
8	CONNECTICUT	'19TH CENTURY CASTLE	5500000
9	MASSACHUSETTS	'18TH CENTURY MANSION	1200000
10	MASSACHUSETTS	'6 ACRE ISLAND WITH MANSION	7500000
11	SOUTH CAROLINA	PLANTATION	3950000
12	ARIZONA	ESTATE WITH POOL AND SPA	555000
13	MONTANA	BEARTOOTH MOUNTAIN RANCH	1975000

14	MONTANA	YELLOWSTONE RIVER RANCH	1500000
15	COSTA RICA	'12 ACRES, OCEAN VIEW, JUNGLE	15000
16	BAHAMAS	'5 ACRE ISLAND WITH MANSION	885000
17	BAHAMAS	'22 ACRES, CARIBBEAN VIEW	95000
18	NEVIS, WEST INDIES	'17TH CENTURY SUGAR MILL	410000

Once the data is entered, you can change its appearance to make it easier to read. The notebook title and column labels, for example, are all left-aligned. Now you will change them to center them in the column.

CHANGING ALIGNMENT

Alignment can be changed using the Object Inspector menu. The procedure is to select the cells, right-click to bring up the Object Inspector menu, and select Alignment. The choices are General, Left, Right, and Center.

Change the alignment for the title "VACATION PARADISE".

1. Right-click on cell B1.
2. Click on Alignment to select it from the list.
3. Click on Center to center the block.
4. Click on OK to make your selection.

The title will be centered. Follow the same procedure to center the column labels.

1. Select the block A3..C3 and right-click.
2. Click on Alignment and Center to center the block.
3. Click on OK to make your selection.

The column labels will be centered.

COMBINING CURRENCY AND COMMA FORMATS

The prices would also be easier to read if they were formatted as currency. You already know how to select the Numeric Format feature; use it now to format the first price in the column (C5) for currency; format the rest of the cells (C6 through C18) for financial (Comma).

First change C5 to Currency format.

74 First Look at Quattro Pro for Windows

1. Right-click on C5.
2. Select Numeric Format, Currency, 2 decimal places.
3. Click on OK to make your selection.

Next change block C6..C18 to Comma format.

1. Select block C6..C18 and right-click.
2. Select Numeric Format, Comma, 2 decimal places.
3. Click on OK to make your selection.

The prices are displayed in Currency and Comma formats (see Figure 5-1).

Figure 5-1
Vacation Paradise data

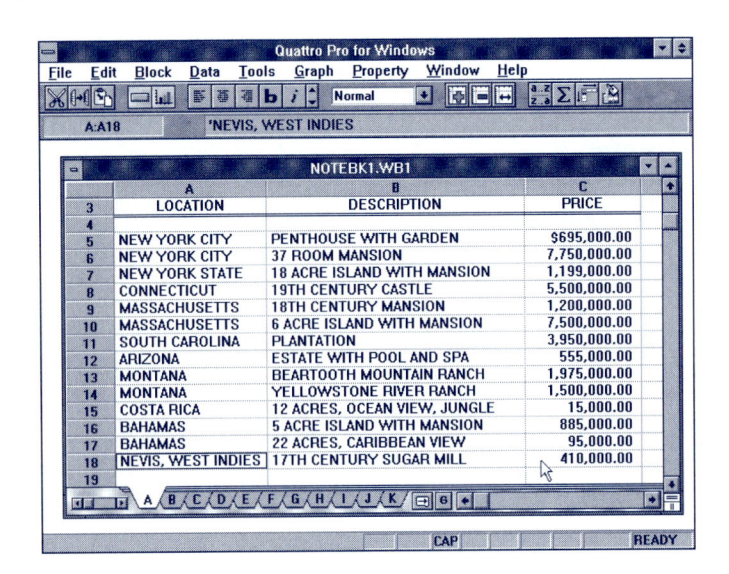

	A	B	C
3	LOCATION	DESCRIPTION	PRICE
4			
5	NEW YORK CITY	PENTHOUSE WITH GARDEN	$695,000.00
6	NEW YORK CITY	37 ROOM MANSION	7,750,000.00
7	NEW YORK STATE	18 ACRE ISLAND WITH MANSION	1,199,000.00
8	CONNECTICUT	19TH CENTURY CASTLE	5,500,000.00
9	MASSACHUSETTS	18TH CENTURY MANSION	1,200,000.00
10	MASSACHUSETTS	6 ACRE ISLAND WITH MANSION	7,500,000.00
11	SOUTH CAROLINA	PLANTATION	3,950,000.00
12	ARIZONA	ESTATE WITH POOL AND SPA	555,000.00
13	MONTANA	BEARTOOTH MOUNTAIN RANCH	1,975,000.00
14	MONTANA	YELLOWSTONE RIVER RANCH	1,500,000.00
15	COSTA RICA	12 ACRES, OCEAN VIEW, JUNGLE	15,000.00
16	BAHAMAS	5 ACRE ISLAND WITH MANSION	885,000.00
17	BAHAMAS	22 ACRES, CARIBBEAN VIEW	95,000.00
18	NEVIS, WEST INDIES	17TH CENTURY SUGAR MILL	410,000.00

USING THE SPEEDSORT BUTTON

There is one last enhancement you can make to the notebook's appearance. As the information is arranged now, there is no obvious order to the rows. It would be easier to use if the entries were arranged in alphabetical order by location. Since sorting rows in alphabetical order is a common activity in notebooks, Quattro Pro for Windows provides a **SpeedSort button** on the SpeedBar (refer to Figure 5-2). The SpeedSort button is designed for quick sorting (we will discuss more complicated sorting in Lesson Six). The procedure for the SpeedSort button is to select the entire block of information you wish to sort, then specify the column or columns you want to sort by. You specify the columns by holding down the Ctrl and Shift keys with one hand while using the mouse to click on the columns with the other. If you do not specify a column to sort by, Quattro Pro for Windows assumes you want to sort by the first column in the block. Once you have selected a block and specified a column, either click on the *upper* half of the SpeedSort button for ascending alphabetical order (A to Z) or the *lower* half for descending alphabetical order (Z to A).

Follow these steps to sort the vacation information in alphabetical order by location:

1. Select all the information you wish to sort (cell block A5..C18). Don't include the column labels or they will be mixed in with the property list.

2. Since Location is the first column in the block, Quattro Pro for Windows will sort the rows by location automatically. Therefore you do not need to specify a column.

3. Click on the upper part of the SpeedSort button. The information will be sorted in ascending alphabetical order by location.

4. Use the Object Inspector menu to change the value at the top of the column to Currency format and the value in C15 to Comma format. The notebook will look like Figure 5-2.

Figure 5-2
Sorted Vacation Paradise notebook

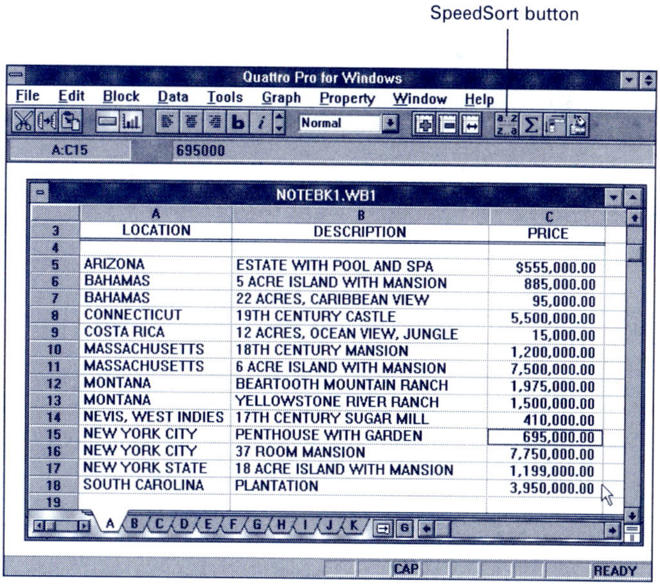

Your spreadsheet notebook is now complete, and you are ready to use Quattro Pro for Windows' functions to analyze your information.

USING THE @COUNT, @MAX, AND @MIN FUNCTIONS

In this lesson, you can easily count the total number of properties in the list and find the highest and lowest priced properties. If you had a very long list, though, or one that changed often, you would find it much harder to obtain those figures by counting. For that reason, Quattro Pro for Windows provides functions to keep track of the information for you. @COUNT(cell block) will count the number of nonblank cells in the specified block. @MAX(cell block) will find the highest value in the specified block. And @MIN(cell block) will find the lowest value in the specified block.

To see how these functions work:

1. Move to A20 and enter the following labels:

	A
20	**Number of Properties:**
21	**Highest Price:**
22	**Lowest Price:**

2. Move to B20 and press [Alt]-[F3] to bring up the Function menu.

3. Select COUNT.

4. Select the block consisting of the list of property locations, A5..A18.

5. Type) to complete the function and press [Enter]. @COUNT shows that there are 14 properties in the specified block, which is correct.

To calculate the maximum price:

1. Move to B21, press [Alt]-[F3] to bring up the Function menu, and select MAX.

2. This time you want to know the maximum price, so select the block consisting of the list of prices, C5..C18.

3. Type) to complete the function and press [Enter]

4. Use the Object Inspector menu to format the cell for Currency, 2 decimal places.

The maximum price on the list is $7,750,000, for the 37-room mansion in New York City.

To calculate the minimum price:

1. Move to B22, press [Alt]-[F3] to bring up the Function menu, and select MIN.

2. Select the block consisting of the list of prices, C5..C18.

3. Type) to complete the function and press [Enter]

4. Use the Object Inspector menu to format the cell for Currency, 2 decimal places.

The minimum price on the list is $15,000, for the 12 acres, ocean view, and jungle in Costa Rica.

Now that you have calculated the number of properties, the highest price, and the lowest price, you can move on to determining monthly payments.

USING THE @PMT FUNCTION

In order to find the monthly payments for each property, you can use Quattro Pro for Windows' built-in @PMT function. @PMT calculates monthly payments given the amount of the loan (the principal), the monthly interest rate, and the number of payment periods (the term). The structure is @PMT(principal, interest rate per period, number of payment periods). Like other Quattro Pro for Windows functions, @PMT allows you to enter values by using cell addresses rather than numbers.

NOTE: @PMT can be adjusted to fit other time periods, for example, quarterly or annual payments; but in that case the interest rate and payment periods must also be quarterly or annual.

To illustrate this feature, assume that you are able to arrange financing for a potential vacation home purchase at 8.5% annual interest over a 30-year period. To make calculation easier, enter the following information in a separate area of the spreadsheet, cells A25 through B27. Note that B26 contains a formula.

	A	B
25	Interest, annual:	.085
26	Interest, monthly:	+B25/12
27	Term (in months):	360

Use Numeric Format to display the values in B25 and B26 in percentages.

1. Select B25..B26 and bring up the Numeric Format menu.

2. Select Percent, 1 decimal place. Click on OK to make your selection.

You will enter the @PMT function into cell C30. Start with the price of the Arizona estate for the principal. The completed function will be @PMT(C5,B26,B27). To enter it:

1. Move to C30.

2. Press [Alt]-[F3] to bring up the Function menu.

3. Select PMT.

4. Click on C5 and type **,**

5. Click on B26 and type **,**

6. Click on B27 and type **)** to complete the function.

7. Press [Enter] to calculate the value.

8. Use Numeric Format to display it as Currency, 2 decimal places. The monthly payment on the Arizona estate is $4267.47.

CREATING LINKS

The last step is to label the monthly payment by property. As usual, you have choices. You could type the name or you could copy the label in A5 to A30. In each case, the new label would have no further connection, or **link,** to the original list. A third possibility, which would create a link, is to enter the cell address of the original label (+A5). That would preserve its connection to the original list and would be especially useful in copying, as we will see later in the lesson. To add the location:

1. Move to cell A30.

2. Type **+A5** and press [Enter]. "ARIZONA" will appear in cell A30.

To copy the description:

1. Move to B30.

2. Type **+B5** and press [Enter]. "ESTATE WITH POOL AND SPA" will appear in cell B30.

COPYING FUNCTIONS

In order to calculate the monthly payments for the other properties, you could redo or edit the function, substituting the cell address for the new property price you wish to calculate. That is, instead of C5 in the function @PMT(C5,B26,B27), you could edit the function to use C6 if you wished to calculate monthly payments for the 5-acre island in the Bahamas, or C12 if you wished to calculate monthly payments for the Beartooth Mountain Ranch in Montana.

A more systematic way to proceed, though, is to copy the function thirteen times, applying it to each of the remaining properties on the list in turn. The procedure is similar to the one you used in the last lesson. First select the cell you wish to copy and then click on the Copy button on the SpeedBar. Then select the cells where you want the copies to go and click on the Paste button. In this case, you want to copy C30, the cell containing the function; you want to copy it to 13 cells, since there are 14 properties in all. As you know, however, copying functions and formulas requires special care to make sure that they continue to refer to the correct cell addresses after they are copied.

Move to C30 and look at the function on the input line. If the function were copied to C31 (one row down), all the cell addresses would also move down one row. C5 would become C6, B26 would become B27, and B27 would become B28. If the function were copied two rows down, the cell addresses would become C7, B28, and B29. In the case of the cell address for the principal of the loan, the change would be useful, because the changing cell addresses would move down the list of properties. In the case of the interest rate and number of payment periods, though, the change would create problems, because the cell addresses in the copied functions would no longer refer to the proper cells. This would result in an error message (ERR) being placed in the cell where the function contained the incorrect cell reference.

To illustrate this, try copying the function in C30 to C31.

1. Move to C30.

2. Click on the Copy button.

3. Move to C31.

4. Click on the Paste button.

The function is copied, but the ERR message appears. Move to C31 if you are not there already and look at the input line to see why. The copied function reads @PMT(C6,B27,B28). Since B27 contains the value 360, Quattro Pro for Windows interprets it as the value to use for the interest rate. (Imagine a monthly interest rate of 360%!) B28 is blank, so Quattro Pro for Windows cannot calculate the result.

5. Press [Del] to delete the incorrect function.

Before it can be copied, then, the function in C30 must be edited so that the cell addresses for interest and payment periods (B27 and B28) are absolute, rather than relative. That way the function will always refer to those two cells, even when it is copied. To change the cell reference to absolute:

1. Move to C30 and press [F2] to edit it.

2. Move the blinking line until it is on the second cell address, B26.

3. Press [F4]. Dollar signs will be inserted and the function will now read "@PMT(C5,$A:$B$26,B27)".

4. Move the cursor to the next cell address in the function (B27) and press [F4]. Again dollar signs will be inserted, so the function will now read "@PMT(C5,$A:$B$26,$A:$B$27)".

80 First Look at Quattro Pro for Windows

5. Press [Enter] to enter the changes to the function. Notice that the displayed value, $4267.47, does not change.

Now you can copy the function in C30 and the links in A30 and B30 to easily calculate monthly payments for all the properties.

1. Move to A30 and select cells A30..C30.

2. Click on the Copy button.

3. Select cells A31..C43.

4. Click on the Paste button.

The labels and functions are copied. The bottom part of the spreadsheet will look like Figure 5-3.

Figure 5-3
Monthly payments for all properties

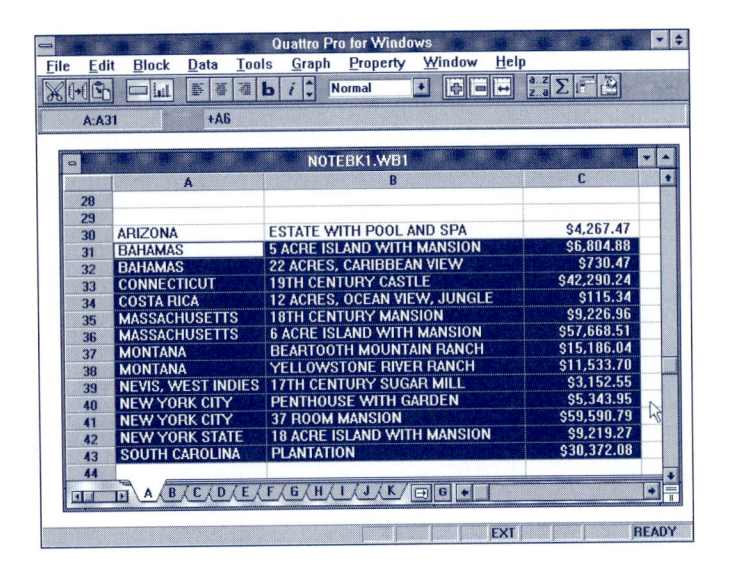

	A	B	C
28			
29			
30	ARIZONA	ESTATE WITH POOL AND SPA	$4,267.47
31	BAHAMAS	5 ACRE ISLAND WITH MANSION	$6,804.88
32	BAHAMAS	22 ACRES, CARIBBEAN VIEW	$730.47
33	CONNECTICUT	19TH CENTURY CASTLE	$42,290.24
34	COSTA RICA	12 ACRES, OCEAN VIEW, JUNGLE	$115.34
35	MASSACHUSETTS	18TH CENTURY MANSION	$9,226.96
36	MASSACHUSETTS	6 ACRE ISLAND WITH MANSION	$57,668.51
37	MONTANA	BEARTOOTH MOUNTAIN RANCH	$15,186.04
38	MONTANA	YELLOWSTONE RIVER RANCH	$11,533.70
39	NEVIS, WEST INDIES	17TH CENTURY SUGAR MILL	$3,152.55
40	NEW YORK CITY	PENTHOUSE WITH GARDEN	$5,343.95
41	NEW YORK CITY	37 ROOM MANSION	$59,590.79
42	NEW YORK STATE	18 ACRE ISLAND WITH MANSION	$9,219.27
43	SOUTH CAROLINA	PLANTATION	$30,372.08
44			

As you can see, for as little as $115.34 or as much as $59,590.79 per month, that vacation paradise you've always wanted can be yours.

Using the Copy and Paste buttons shows the advantage of using cell addresses to display the location and description of each property. If the labels had been retyped or copied as labels, each one would have had to be retyped or recopied. Instead the single Copy and Paste commands recreated the entire list.

This spreadsheet notebook, like all others, will rapidly recalculate formulas when values are changed. To see this, assume that you can find an interest rate of 7.5%, rather than 8.5%.

1. Move to cell B25.

2. Change the value to .075 and press [Enter]

The monthly payments for all properties are automatically recalculated.

USING THE @IF FUNCTION

The method of developing functions and copying them works well if you have a limited number of specific options to analyze. In many cases though, the choices are not as clear-cut. The question you want to ask may not be "What are the monthly payments for this property," but rather, "Since I can afford up to a certain amount for monthly payments, what price range should I be looking in?" For that question, you can use the @IF function, which allows you to set up a condition. If the condition is met, Quattro Pro for Windows will insert a specified value, label, or formula. If it is not met, Quattro Pro for Windows will insert a different value, label, or formula. The function has the structure @IF(condition, what to do if condition is met, what to do if it is not met).

Assume that you feel it is too difficult to look over the list of monthly payments and decide which ones are less than your desired payment. You can use @IF to set up a conditional statement: If the payment on the list is less than the desired payment, "YES" will be entered. If it is more, "NO" will be entered. To see how this works, assume you wish to pay no more than $5000 per month. The condition for the function is therefore "monthly payment<5000". You can make the task easier by first entering the value for the desired payment into a cell.

1. Move to A28. Type **Desired payment:** and press [Enter]

2. Move to B28. Type **5000** and press [Enter]

3. Use Numeric Format to display the value in B28 in Currency format, 2 decimal places.

Now you are ready to enter the function for the first property on the list, the Arizona estate.

1. Move to D30.

2. Press [Alt]-[F3] to bring up the Function menu.

3. Select IF.

4. Click on the first monthly payment at C30.

5. Type < (less than).

6. Click on the desired payment, B28.

7. Press [F4] to make it an absolute cell reference.

8. Type **,**

9. Type **"YES"**

10. Type **,**

82   First Look at Quattro Pro for Windows

11. Type **"NO"**

12. Type **)** and press [Enter] to complete the function. YES appears in D30.

Look at the function on the input line, @IF(C30<$A:$B$28,"YES","NO"). It says that if the value in C30 is less than the value in B28, YES should be entered into the cell. If not, NO should be entered. C30 is a relative cell reference while B28 is an absolute cell reference, so that the function can easily be copied for all the monthly payments on the list. The quotation marks around YES and NO in the function let Quattro Pro for Windows know you are typing a word, not a cell reference. They do not appear in the cell, as you can see.

Copy the function in D30 to D31..D43. When done, the bottom of the spreadsheet should look like Figure 5-4.

Figure 5-4
The @IF function

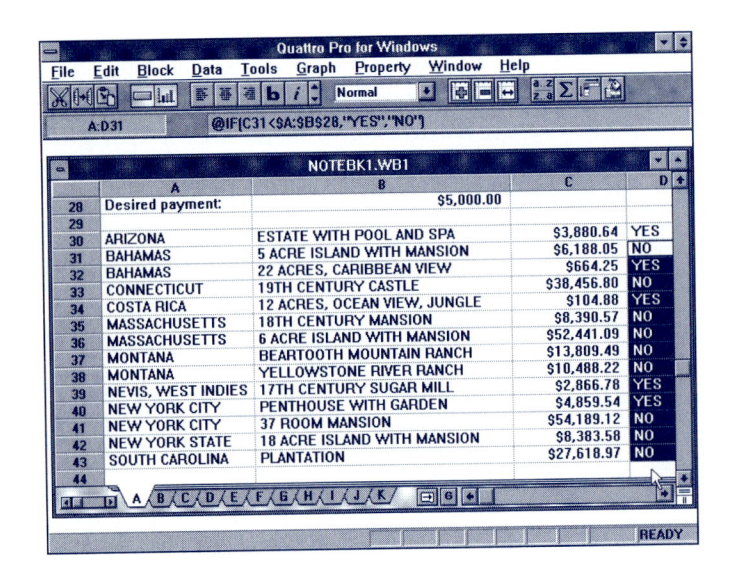

You have now completed the Vacation Paradise notebook. Save it as VACATION.WB1. Then exit Quattro Pro for Windows.

■ SUMMARY OF COMMANDS

Topic or Feature	Command or Reference	Menu	Page
Column Width	Right-click on the cell or block to be modified, then click on Column Width; or use the Fit button on the SpeedBar	Object Inspector menus	71

Topic or Feature	Command or Reference	Menu	Page
Select a Block	Shift-F7		72
Alignment of Labels	Right-click on the cell or block to be modified, then click on Alignment; or use the Alignment buttons on the SpeedBar	Object Inspector menus	73
Comma (Financial) Format	Right-click on the cell or block to be modified, then click on Numeric Format, Comma	Object Inspector menus	73
Sort a Block	Select block, then click on the SpeedSort button on the SpeedBar		74
Count Cells in a Block	@COUNT(); Alt-F3, select COUNT		76
Maximum Value in a Block	@MAX(); Alt-F3, select MAX		76
Minimum Value in a Block	@MIN(); Alt-F3, select MIN		76
Percent Format	Right-click on the cell or block to be modified, then click on Numeric Format, Percent	Object Inspector menus	77
Loan Payments	@PMT(); Alt-F3, select PMT		77
Conditional Statements	@IF(); Alt-F3, select IF		81

■ REVIEW QUESTIONS

1. How do you specify column width?
2. How do you select a block using the keyboard?
3. What steps would you follow to display cell contents in Comma format? Percent format?
4. What steps would you follow to right-align cell contents? To center cell contents?
5. Describe the purpose of the following functions: @COUNT, @MAX, @MIN, @PMT.

6. What is a conditional statement? Why would you want to use one in a spreadsheet?

7. What function would you use to set up a conditional statement? What information must it include?

8. You are at cell A14. What would you enter to create a link with the value in A1, so that if A1 changed, A14 would change as well?

9. You want to set up a conditional statement in B3 to find out whether a value in cell B6 is equal to one-third your weekly salary. If it is, you want to display the word "Eureka!" If it is not, you want to display the word "Oops!" How would you write the statement?

■ HANDS-ON EXERCISES

Use the following data for all three exercises:

Acura	Legend	$26,945
Dodge	Van	$16,989
Jeep	Cherokee	$16,550
Isuzu	Pickup	$8,144
Plymouth	Sundance	$8,966
Chrysler	New Yorker	$14,379
Ford	Probe	$12,735
Honda	Accord	$11,995
Subaru	Legacy	$12,995
Hyundai	Excel	$6,799

Exercise 5-1 Create a spreadsheet notebook to analyze these car prices. Be sure to include labels to identify all your calculations.

1. Enter a title for the notebook. Enter the car make, the model, and the price in separate columns. Give each column a label.

2. Adjust the column widths as necessary and use Line Draw to enhance the appearance of the notebook.

3. Center each column title.

4. Use functions to calculate the most expensive car and the least expensive car.

5. Quattro Pro for Windows has a function @AVG(), which calculates the average of a block of cells. Its structure is AVG(cell block). Use it to calculate the average car price.

6. Calculate monthly loan payments on each car, assuming an 8.5% annual interest rate and a 4-year loan.

7. Assume that you want to pay no more than $350 per month. Use @IF to calculate which car payments you can afford.

8. Save the notebook as CARS1.WB1.

Exercise 5-2

This exercise builds on Exercise 5-1. Assume that you intend to use the car you purchase entirely for business purposes. You therefore want to write it off on your tax return as a deduction. You must do this over a 6-year period. The depreciation schedule you will use is:

1st year	20%
2nd year	32%
3rd year	19.2%
4th year	11.52%
5th year	11.52%
6th year	5.76%

The depreciation deduction each year is the percentage multiplied by the price of the car.

Calculate the depreciation deduction for each car over the 6-year period.

1. Create a list of car make, model, and prices in a blank section of the spreadsheet using cell addresses to create links. Be sure to include labels for each column.

2. Quattro Pro for Windows has a SpeedFill button on the SpeedBar that automatically enters items in a series. You can use it to enter column labels for the deductions for the 1st year through the 6th year. Enter **'1st Year** in the cell to the right of the label for prices. Then select a block consisting of the "1st Year" label plus the five cells to the right in that row. Finally click on SpeedFill. The rest of the labels through "6th Year" will be entered.

3. Enter the deduction schedule for each car in the appropriate cells. *Hint*: Enter the depreciation schedule in a blank section of the spreadsheet and use formulas with absolute cell addresses to refer to it.

4. Save the notebook as CARS2.WB1.

Exercise 5-3

This exercise builds on Exercise 5-1. Quattro Pro for Windows includes a feature called Solve For on the Tools menu. It allows you to work backwards from the desired result of a formula to the conditions needed to produce that result. Clicking on Solve For displays a dialog box. You must specify three pieces of information: the Formula Cell (the cell where the formula is located), the Target Value (the desired result of the formula), and the Variable Cell (the cell where the result of Solve For should be placed).

Assume that you want to keep loan payments below $350 per month. Use Solve For to work backwards to find the maximum car price you can afford.

1. In a blank section of the notebook, set up the formula cell containing the @PMT function. It should use cell addresses to refer to the interest rate and payment periods you entered in Exercise 5-1. It should use the cell address of a blank cell for the loan principal; that cell address is the variable cell. The target value is 500.

2. Label the formula cell and the variable cell.

3. Click on Solve For, enter the information in the edit fields, and click on OK.

4. Change the target value to 200 and recalculate the loan principal.

5. Change the target value to 500 and recalculate the loan principal.

6. Save the notebook as CARS3.WB1.

LESSON SIX: Creating a Database

OBJECTIVES

At the end of this lesson, you will be able to:
- Design a database in Quattro Pro for Windows.
- Fill a block with sequential values.
- Assign names to database fields.
- Sort a database.
- Set up search criteria to find specific records.
- Locate database records that meet specific criteria.
- Extract database records that meet specific criteria and copy them to a new section of the notebook.
- Reset Data | Query.
- Use Point mode to select a block from a dialog box.

DESIGNING A DATABASE

For many spreadsheet applications, you can analyze data simply by organizing it into rows and columns. But in some cases you will need other kinds of tools to manipulate data. You may have to sort it according to the information in specific columns or search through it to find data that fits certain criteria. For these situations, you must set up your data as a database—a collection of information organized into fields (also called "variables") and records.

The most common example of a database is a personal address book. Each person or company in it—each separate entry—is a **record**. Each piece of information in the record—name, address, telephone number—is a **field**. Most address books are organized according to the last names or the company names of the entries. In database jargon, that sentence would read: "Most address databases are sorted on the **key field** of last or company name." An ordinary address book can be arranged in only one order (sorted on one key field), unless you cut it apart and rearrange it. The same addresses, when placed in a database on a computer, could be sorted on last name, first name, zip code, street address, or whatever field you specify. The computer can also search for a specified name or find all entries with a specified area code much more quickly than you can.

Some computer programs are designed specifically to handle databases. Although Quattro Pro for Windows is not a pure database program, it includes some of the most useful features of a database together with its powerful spreadsheet capabilities. You can define records and fields, sort on a key field, and search for records in which certain fields meet certain criteria.

In designing a database, you must keep in mind how Quattro Pro for Windows expects records and fields to be entered. Each *record* should fit on one row, with each *field* placed in a separate column of that row. For example, if you wished to enter the information from your personal address book into a Quattro Pro for Windows database, you would enter the name, address, and telephone number all on the same row, rather than on separate rows, as they might be in your address book. "Last Name" might be one field, and all last names would have to be entered in the same column, for example, column A. All first names might be entered in column B, all street addresses in C, all cities in D, all states in E, all countries in F, and all telephone numbers in G. You could then assign names to each column and refer to those names when sorting or searching the database. The advantage of using Quattro Pro for Windows, rather than a database program, is that the cells and columns can still be manipulated and used in spreadsheet calculations. You can also use the editing and analysis tools you learned in previous lessons.

To illustrate Quattro Pro for Windows' database features, you will create an application using a database based on the sales records of a bookstore. Assume that information on each book in stock, including title, price, and unit sales (updated monthly), has been kept on index cards. Sales have grown to the point that you, as store manager, want a more efficient way of keeping track of them than crossing out the old unit sales figures and writing in the new ones each month. You would also like to quickly calculate total sales, sort records, and search through records without having to shuffle many boxes of index cards. Therefore you decide to enter the information into a Quattro Pro for Windows database.

Setting up a database requires careful planning. Follow these instructions and refer to Figure 6-1 to enter the data:

1. Since each column must contain a separate field of the database, you should make columns wide enough to hold each field. The fields will be TITLE, PRICE, UNIT SALES, and TOTAL SALES. Use the Object Inspector menu to expand columns A through D to the following widths:

Column	Width
A	25
B	12
C	12
D	15

2. For the title of the notebook, move to A1. Type **BOOKSTORE SALES** and press Enter

3. In cells A3 through D3, enter the following labels for the database fields:

Cell	Label
A3	**TITLE**
B3	**PRICE**
C3	**UNIT SALES**
D3	**TOTAL SALES**

4. Select A3..D3 and use the Object Inspector menu to align the titles in the center of the cells.

5. In cells A4 through C13, enter the following data:

	A	B	C
4	Man Without a Condo	5.95	400
5	Little Persons	6.95	700
6	Ashley in Wonderland	5.95	750
7	'1001 Ways to Live Forever	7.95	800
8	Raspberry Swede	9.95	975
9	Recycling Murders	9.95	875
10	Royal Family at Home	8.95	350
11	Barbecue League Baseball	6.95	1200
12	Moby Fred	12.00	1175
13	Gone With the Cold Front	10.00	1050

6. Column D, TOTAL SALES, should contain PRICE multiplied by UNIT SALES.

   a. Move to D4.

   b. Enter the following formula, using techniques you learned in earlier lessons: **+B4*C4**

   c. Use the Copy and Paste SpeedBar buttons to copy the formula in D4 to cells D5 through D13.

7. Finally use the Object Inspector menu to display the values in the PRICE and TOTAL SALES columns (B4..B13 and D4..D13) in Currency format, 2 decimal places.

The notebook should look like Figure 6-1.

Filling a Block with Sequential Values

The data entry for the database is complete. Before using the Quattro Pro for Windows commands to define it as a database, though, you should learn a useful editing technique called Block | Fill, which lets you to fill a block with sequential values. It is especially useful in a database because you can assign

Figure 6-1
Bookstore Sales notebook

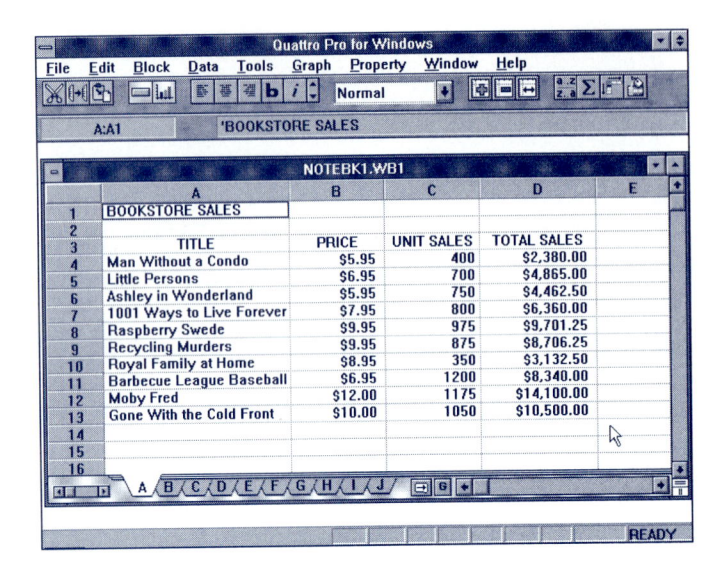

[Screenshot of Quattro Pro for Windows showing the BOOKSTORE SALES notebook with columns TITLE, PRICE, UNIT SALES, and TOTAL SALES for various book titles.]

an identification number to each record. Assume that you want to assign each record a number, starting with 1 for *Man Without a Condo*. These identification numbers will be assigned to a new field, NUMBER. You will place the identification number in a column to the left of the book title.

Insert a new column to hold the field.

1. Select column A.

2. Click on the Insert button on the SpeedBar.

3. Move to A3. Type **NUMBER** and press [Enter]

You are now ready to fill cells A4 through A13 with sequential values, starting with 1.

1. Select A4..A13.

2. Select Block | Fill. A dialog box appears (see Figure 6-2).

The block you specified appears in the Blocks edit field; other edit fields prompt you for the **Start value,** the **Step value,** and the **Stop value.** The Start value is the first number of the sequence, the Step value is the amount by which to increase each cell, and the Stop value is the last number of the sequence. Quattro Pro for Windows starts out by assuming that the Start value will be 0, the Step value will be 1, and the Stop value will be 8191, but you can enter any number or formula into the boxes.

In this case, you want to set the Start value to 1 and keep the Step value at 1, so that the sequence will be 1,2,3... (If you chose 1 for the Start value and 10 for the Step value, the sequence would be 1,11,21...) Since you have already specified a block, you need not change the Stop value: Quattro Pro for Windows will stop when it reaches either the end of the specified block or the default number, 8191, whichever comes first.

Figure 6-2
Filling a block with sequential values

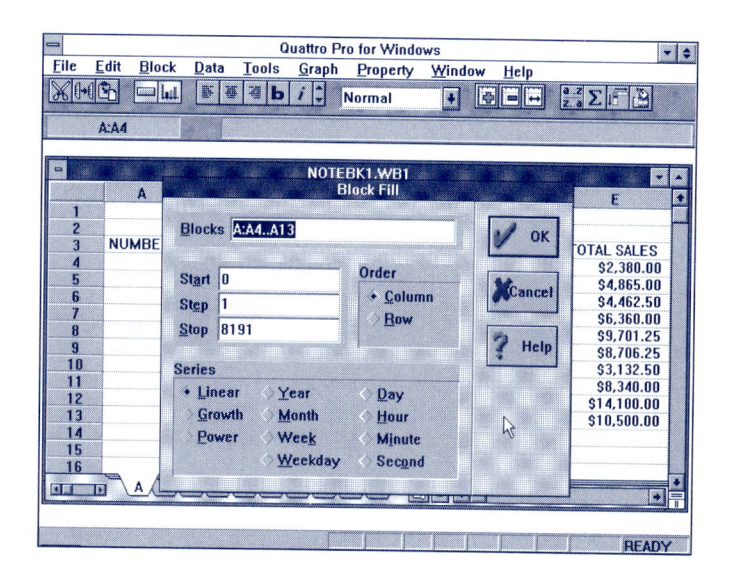

3. Click on the OK button. The cell block will be filled with sequential values.

This technique is especially useful for entering a long sequence of order numbers. To demonstrate this, assume that the book data was entered in the order of the original purchase order numbers, which began at 12345.

1. Select Block ¦ Fill. Quattro Pro for Windows remembers the last block you specified, so you need not specify it again.

2. Click on the Start edit field (or press Tab). Delete "1" and type **12345**

3. Click on the Stop value box (or press Tab twice). Delete "8191" and type 50000. You cannot leave the Stop value as 8191 in this case, because it is less than 12345. Remember, Quattro Pro for Windows will stop at the end of the specified block, or at the displayed Stop value, whichever comes first.

4. Click on the OK button. Again the block will be filled with sequential values, starting at 12345.

Assigning Names to Fields

Now you are ready to assign names to your fields. You of course already know what the field names are (NUMBER, TITLE, PRICE, UNIT SALES, and TOTAL SALES). But for Quattro Pro for Windows to recognize the names, you have to use the Data ¦ Query ¦ Field Names command. For this command to work, you must always set up your database as you have done in this application: one record per row, each field in a separate column, and no lines or blank rows between the field names and field data.

To assign names to fields, define the block that contains the database, then select Data | Query, click on the Field Names button, and click on Close.

NOTE: You can also select Data|Query first, then specify the block by typing it into the Database Block section of the dialog box.

1. Select A3..E13.
2. Select Data | Query. A dialog box appears (see Figure 6-3). The block you have specified appears in the Database Block field of the dialog box.

Figure 6-3
Assigning names to database fields

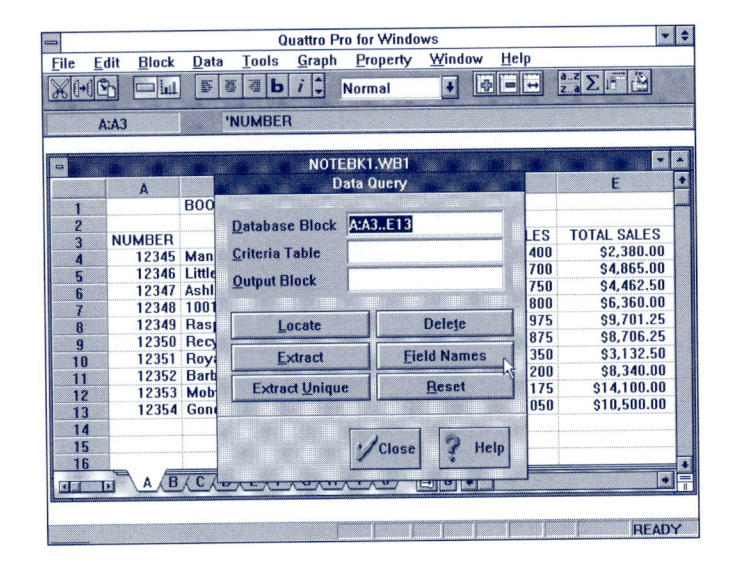

3. Click on the Field Names button.
4. Click on Close to exit the dialog box and return to the notebook.

SORTING THE DATABASE

Assume you want to sort the books in alphabetical order by title to make it easier for your staff to find information. As with other Quattro Pro for Windows commands, you must specify the block containing the cells you wish to sort, in this case the entire database. The block must include all rows and columns that make up the database, but it must *not* include the field titles. Then select Data | Sort, specify the sort key or keys, and click on OK.

NOTE: You can also select Data!Sort first, then specify the block by typing it into the Block section of the dialog box.

1. Select A4..E13.

2. Select Data | Sort. A dialog box appears (see Figure 6-4). The block you have selected appears in the Block field of the dialog box.

3. Click on the "1st" edit field and type **TITLE**

Figure 6-4
Sorting a database

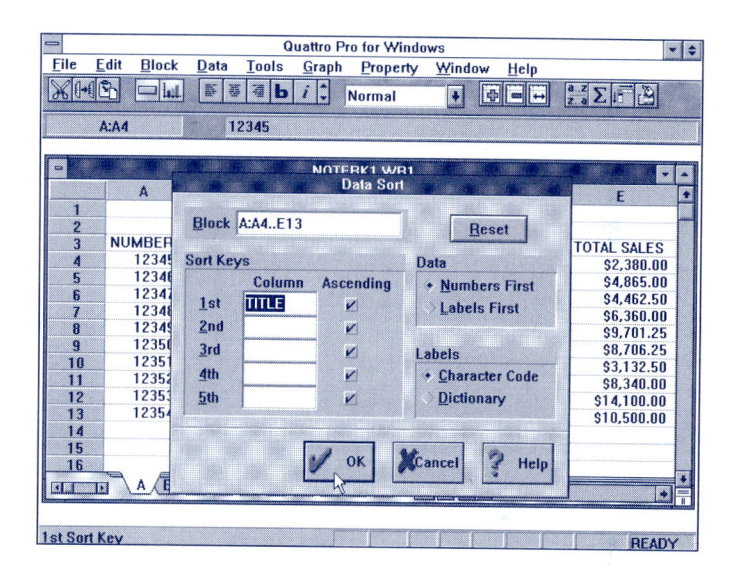

Quattro Pro for Windows assumes you want to sort in ascending order; if you did not, you would click the Ascending button to remove the check (✔).

4. Click on the OK button. The database is sorted in alphabetical order by title.

Oh no! You've just realized that your only complete set of inventory records on index cards is in order of NUMBER. You have to be able to check each record in the computer database against its index card, but now that you've sorted it in alphabetical order, that's impossible to do. It would take weeks to alphabetize all those index cards so that they match the current form of the computer database. Fortunately you have guarded against this by including the identification number as one of the database fields; so you can easily organize the computer database in order of NUMBER again.

5. Re-sort, using Data | Sort and typing NUMBER as the 1st key field. When you have finished, the database should once again be in order of NUMBER.

LOCATING RECORDS IN A DATABASE

Databases are shown to their best advantage when used to quickly find or extract data. To see how this feature works, assume that you want to find the books for which total sales are less than $5000, in order to make them part of a sales drive. You can do this by first setting up a **criteria table,** a block of cells that sets the criteria for the search. A criteria table must include two pieces of information: the field to be searched and the criteria to be used in selecting the record. Each criterion is always placed in the cell below the field. You can then use the Data ¦ Query dialog box either to search the database to locate those records that fit the criteria or to place copies of the records in a specially designated area called the **output block.**

Begin the process by setting up the criteria table. In this case, the field is TOTAL SALES and the criterion is a formula, TOTAL SALES<5000.

1. Label the criteria table.

    a. Move to B15.

    b. Type **Criteria Table:** and press [Enter]

2. Enter the field to be searched.

    a. Move to B16.

    b. Type **TOTAL SALES** and press [Enter]

3. Enter the criterion.

    a. Move to B17.

    b. Type **+TOTAL SALES<5000** and press [Enter]. The plus sign lets Quattro Pro for Windows know you are typing a formula; if you leave it out, the program will assume you are typing a label.

The criteria table is set up. You are now ready to search the database using Locate.

1. Select Data ¦ Query. This brings up the Query dialog box again. Notice that the block A3..E13 is still defined from the Field Names command. Since you will use the same block in this command, you do not need to redefine it.

2. Click on Criteria Table (or press [Tab]).

3. Type **B16..B17** (the cell block of your criteria table).

4. Click on the Locate button. Quattro Pro for Windows will highlight the first record to match the criterion (see Figure 6-5).

5. Press [↓] to find the other records.

Figure 6-5
Locating records that meet specified criteria

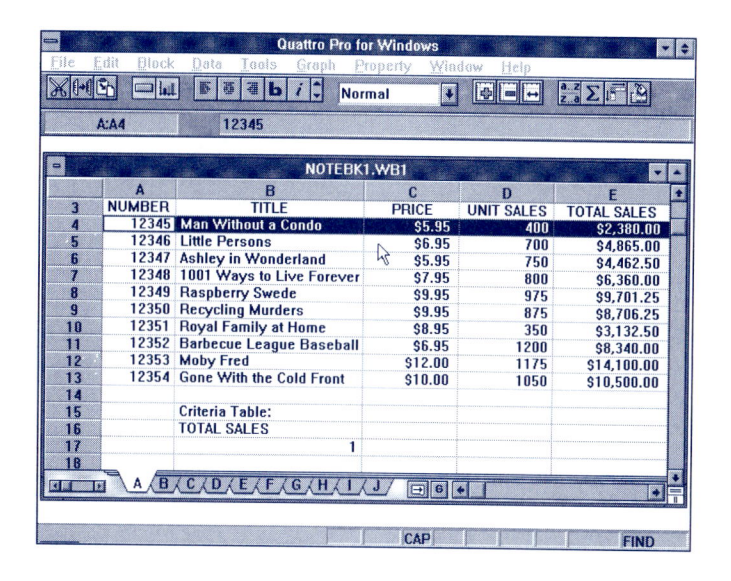

	A	B	C	D	E
3	NUMBER	TITLE	PRICE	UNIT SALES	TOTAL SALES
4	12345	Man Without a Condo	$5.95	400	$2,380.00
5	12346	Little Persons	$6.95	700	$4,865.00
6	12347	Ashley in Wonderland	$5.95	750	$4,462.50
7	12348	1001 Ways to Live Forever	$7.95	800	$6,360.00
8	12349	Raspberry Swede	$9.95	975	$9,701.25
9	12350	Recycling Murders	$9.95	875	$8,706.25
10	12351	Royal Family at Home	$8.95	350	$3,132.50
11	12352	Barbecue League Baseball	$6.95	1200	$8,340.00
12	12353	Moby Fred	$12.00	1175	$14,100.00
13	12354	Gone With the Cold Front	$10.00	1050	$10,500.00
14					
15		Criteria Table:			
16		TOTAL SALES			
17		1			

Go through the database to see all the records that meet the criteria. When you reach the end:

6. Press [Esc] to return to the Data | Query box.
7. Click on Close to return to the notebook.

EXTRACTING RECORDS FROM A DATABASE

Locating records that meet certain criteria can be useful, but for working with them more carefully, you should extract them to a separate part of the database, the output block. You use the criteria table to extract records as well as to locate them. You must also set up the output block, the block of cells where you want the extracted data to go. In addition, you must specify which fields you want included in the output block. Do this by typing the field names you want extracted in the columns where you want them to be placed. You must also let Quattro Pro for Windows know where the output block is by specifying it in the Data | Query box. In this example, you will use the already defined criteria table. All you have to do, therefore, is set up and specify the output block.

1. Move to B18. Type **Output Block:** and press [↓]
2. Move to B19. Type **TITLE** and press [→]
3. Move to C19. Type **PRICE** and press [Enter]

96 First Look at Quattro Pro for Windows

Quattro Pro for Windows will place the title and price information of the books that meet the search criterion directly underneath, starting at row 20.

> **CAUTION:** *Quattro Pro for Windows will overwrite any existing information in the cells designated as the output block, so be sure to place output blocks in a blank area of the notebook.*

Follow these steps to extract the records that fit the criterion:

1. Select Data | Query. The Database Block and Criteria Table should still be specified.
2. Click on Output Block and type **B19..C19**
3. Click on Extract.
4. Click on Close.

The titles and prices of the books that meet the criterion are listed in cells B20 through C23 (see Figure 6-6).

Figure 6-6
Extracting records that meet specified criteria

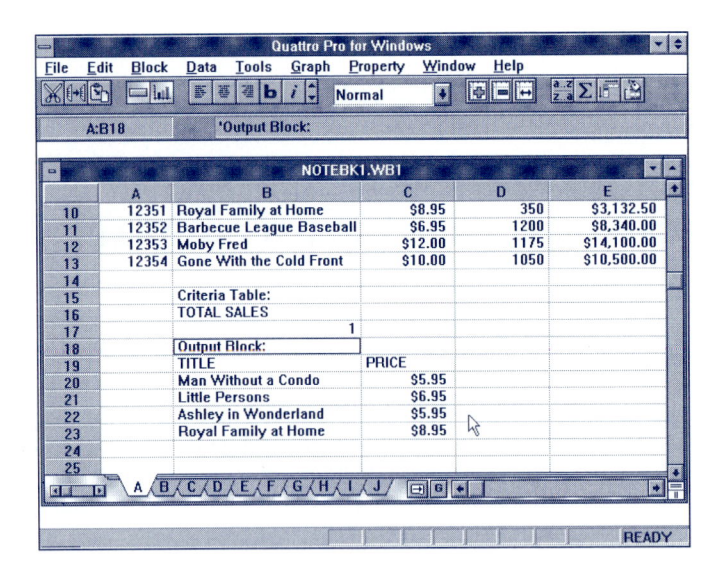

RESETTING DATA | QUERY

As you have seen, Quattro Pro for Windows makes it easy for you to carry out a number of queries using the same database block or criteria table by remembering the blocks you entered in a previous query. Sometimes, though, you may need to change the blocks for the database, the criteria table, or the output block. You can modify the cell blocks by clicking on the appropriate box in the Data ¦ Query dialog box and editing entries. But it is sometimes useful to remove all the entries from a previous query and start over. For this reason, Quattro Pro for Windows provides the **Reset** button on the Data ¦ Query dialog box. Click on it to reset all the Data ¦ Query blocks.

Follow these steps to reset all previous query blocks:

1. Select Data ¦ Query.

2. Click on the Reset button.

3. Click on Close. The entries will be reset.

USING POINT MODE IN DIALOG BOXES

While specifying the cell blocks for criteria tables and output blocks in the Data ¦ Query dialog box, you may have wondered what to do if you happen to forget where you placed them in the notebook. Like other dialog boxes in Quattro Pro for Windows, this one hides most of the notebook. Do you really have to write down or memorize the location of the criteria table and output blocks?

Of course you don't: Quattro Pro for Windows provides a technique, called **Point mode,** for pointing to cell blocks without having to type them. You can use this technique every time you are asked to specify a cell address or block in a dialog box. Instead of clicking *once* on the field and typing the cell address, double-click on it. The dialog box is reduced to its title bar, and you can use the mouse or keyboard to select a block. The cell address of the selected bar will appear on the dialog box title bar. Once you have selected the block, click on the Maximize button on the dialog box title bar to return to the dialog box.

Try this technique now to enter the cell blocks for the database queries you just carried out.

1. Select Data ¦ Query.

2. Double-click on the Database Block field. The dialog box will be reduced to the title bar and the notebook page will be displayed.

3. Select A3..E13.

4. Click on the Maximize button on the dialog box title bar.

5. Double-click on the Criteria Table field, select B16..B17, and click on the Maximize button on the dialog box title bar.

6. Double-click on the Output Block field, select B19..C19, and click on the Maximize button on the dialog box title bar.

7. Click on the Close button to leave the Data | Query dialog box.

Using Point mode makes it easy to enter cell blocks in dialog boxes without typing.

You have now been introduced to Quattro Pro for Windows' database features. Save the notebook as BOOK.WB1 and exit Quattro Pro for Windows.

■ SUMMARY OF COMMANDS

Topic or Feature	Command or Reference	Menu	Page
Sequential Values		Block	Fill	89
Assign Names to Database Fields	Field Names button	Data	Query	91
Sort a Database		Data	Sort	92
Sort Keys	1st through 5th edit fields	Data	Sort	92
Locate Records That Meet Specified Criteria	Locate button	Data	Query	94
Criteria Table	Criteria Table edit field	Data	Query	94
Extract Records That Meet Specified Criteria	Extract button	Data	Query	95
Output Block	Output Block edit field	Data	Query	95
Reset Data Query	Reset button	Data	Query	96
Enter Blocks in Edit Fields with Point Mode	Double-click on the edit field		97

■ REVIEW QUESTIONS

1. How is information organized in a database?

2. How must information be organized in a Quattro Pro for Windows database?

3. When is it useful to fill a block with sequential values?

4. What three pieces of information must you give Quattro Pro for Windows to fill a block with sequential values?

5. What is the purpose of the Field Names button on the Data ¦ Query dialog box?

6. What is a key field? When must you use it?

7. What is a criteria table?

8. List and briefly describe the purpose of two commands from the Data ¦ Query dialog box that require a criteria table.

9. What is an output block?

10. What steps must you follow to enter a block into an edit field using Point mode?

■ HANDS-ON EXERCISES

Exercise 6-1

In this exercise, you will create a database of business contacts. Use the following list of names, businesses, telephone numbers, and appointment days. Remember to type an apostrophe before the telephone numbers to keep them from being entered as numbers.

Ruth Collins	Colonial Paper	637-2777	Thursday
Chris Cominetto	Sojourn Travel	963-4585	Thursday
James Fisher	The Shipping Depot	845-9238	Wednesday
Adam Sherlock	Little Bo-Tique	795-1509	Tuesday
Jeanne Mitman	Mitman Hardware	423-6691	Monday
Gregory Bauer	Office Electronics	854-4112	Friday
Ellen Walsh	The Batter's Box	854-3779	Monday
Tony Silvanio	Sinclair Moving	234-8254	Tuesday
Mary Passarella	Great Scott Fencing	546-5303	Thursday
Michael O'Donnell	Beau Porcelain	547-7885	Thursday

1. Set up a Quattro Pro for Windows database with this data. Include labels for each column and assign them to your database as field names. *Hint:* Enter the names as last name, first name.

2. Add an identification number to each record.

3. Sort the database by last name and company.

4. Print the database.

5. Extract the name, company, and telephone number for all your Thursday appointments. The formula to use in your criteria table is +[field name for appointment days]="Thursday". For example, if you had used the field name Days for your appointment days column, the formula would be +Days="Thursday".

6. Print the list of Thursday appointments.

7. Save the file with the name CONTACT.WB1.

Exercise 6-2

You are planning to purchase new laser printers for your office and have to decide which brand to get. Use the following list of manufacturers, printers, speed in pages per minute (ppm), price, and warranty information.

Brother	HL-10V	4	$1,595	1 year
C-Tech	ProWriter	8	$1,695	1 year
Epson	Action Laser	8	$999	2 years
Epson	EPL-8000	10	$1,999	2 years
Hewlett-Packard	LaserJet IIIP	4	$1,595	1 year
Hewlett-Packard	LaserJet IIP	4	$1,249	1 year
Konica	LP-3110	8	$1,995	1 year
NEC	Silentwriter	10	$1,749	1 year
Okidata	OL 810	8	$1,699	1 year
Panasonic	KX-P4430	5	$1,495	1 year
Star	LaserPrinter	5	$1,395	2 years
Texas Instruments	MicroLaser	6	$1,399	1 year

1. Set up a Quattro Pro for Windows database with the printer information. Use the spreadsheet skills you have learned to present the information as clearly as possible.

2. You would like a list of all the printers under $1700 that print at least 6 ppm. You therefore have to set up a criteria table with two conditions, price < $1700 *and* speed > 5, both of which must be met. This is known as an AND condition, since both the first *and* the second must be met. This criteria table is in effect a combination of two separate criteria tables, one of which contains a formula for price and the other of which contains a formula for speed. Since both conditions must be met, both criteria must be placed on the *same row*, just underneath their respective fields. Use this method to extract and print a list of the printers under $1700 that print at least 6 ppm.

3. Save the notebook as PRINTER.WB1.

Exercise 6-3

This exercise builds on Exercise 6-2. Cost and print speed are two factors that must be considered in your purchase, but reliability and maintenance are other factors. You would like to print a list of printers that either cost less than $1700 and print at least 6 ppm *or* are especially reliable. The criteria for reliability is a 2-year warranty. This condition is known as an OR condition.

You have to set up a criteria table with three conditions to extract the short list of printers. You do this by joining three individual criteria tables. All three field names should be on the same row. Since the first two criteria are joined by an AND condition (that is, they both must be met), the formulas are placed on the same row. The third is joined by an OR condition, so the formula must be entered *one row below* the other two.

1. Use this method to extract and print a list of the printers that either cost $1700 and print at least 6 ppm or have a 2-year warranty.

2. Save the notebook as PRINTER.WB1.

LESSON SEVEN: Creating Graphs

OBJECTIVES

At the end of this lesson, you will be able to:

- Create floating graphs and insert them in the notebook using the Graph tool on the SpeedBar.
- Change the graph type.
- Print a floating graph.
- Create graphs using the Graph menu on the menu bar.
- Edit series.
- Add text.
- View a graph from the Graphs page.
- Name a graph from the Graphs page.
- Use Object Inspector menus to add series labels.
- Print a graph.

You've been working hard all week to get a report ready for your boss. You've arranged all the facts and figures in tidy columns, using lines and boxes to enhance the impact of the most important information. Friday morning you go into the main office to deliver the report. The boss leafs through it, then hands it back and says, "Great job, but I'm too busy to go through all these figures. Tell you what. Why don't you draw me a picture of it. And get it back to me by Monday morning."

Your boss is not unusual in preferring one picture to a thousand spreadsheets. According to one study, presentations using visual aids like charts and graphs were 43% more persuasive than presentations without them. Fortunately you've created the report using Quattro Pro for Windows, so you don't have to run down to the corner drugstore to pick up a ruler and compass and then spend all weekend trying to "draw a picture" of your data. Instead you can use Quattro Pro for Windows' graphing tools to create whatever kinds of charts you need. Quattro Pro for Windows' graphing tools are among its most impressive features and have been praised in reviews of the software. In this lesson, you will be introduced to Quattro Pro for Windows' basic graphing tools: the **Graph tool** on the SpeedBar and the **Graph menu** on the menu bar. You will create **bar graphs** and **pie charts** to show comparisons and **line graphs** to plot relationships among sets of data.

CREATING A GRAPH WITH THE GRAPH TOOL

Some graphs depend on information that is very easy to interpret. Imagine, for example, that you want to create a graph showing market share for your company and your closest competitor. You've made 6873 thingummies in the past year, while your competitor has made 200. This is very easy for you to graph with Quattro Pro for Windows: First select the block of cells containing the information, then click on the *Graph tool* on the SpeedBar (refer to Figure 7-1). The mouse pointer will change to a small graph symbol. Then use the mouse to place the graph in the notebook.

Using a blank spreadsheet, follow these directions to create the graph:

1. Enter this data:

	A	B
1	**US**	6873
2	**THEM**	200

2. Select A1..B2.

3. Click on the Graph tool on the SpeedBar. Then move the mouse pointer back to the notebook. The pointer will change to a small graph symbol.

4. Move the graph symbol to A4, press the left mouse button, drag the mouse until the graph symbol extends through D16, then release the mouse button. A *bar graph* will appear in the notebook, displaying a comparison between your company's thingummy production and your competitor's.

This graph shows clearly that your company made many more thingummies than your competitor. But you can make an even clearer statement by changing the graph type to a *pie chart*, which would display both your company's thingummy production and your competitor's as percentages of total thingummy production. You can do this by using the *Graph menu* on the menu bar.

CHANGING THE GRAPH TYPE

Quattro Pro for Windows allows you to draw many types of graphs: bar, rotated bar, line, X-Y, pie, and 3-D. To change the graph type:

1. Select Graph | Type. The menu in Figure 7-1 will be displayed, showing the various types of graphs Quattro Pro for Windows can draw.

104   First Look at Quattro Pro for Windows

Figure 7-1
Graph types

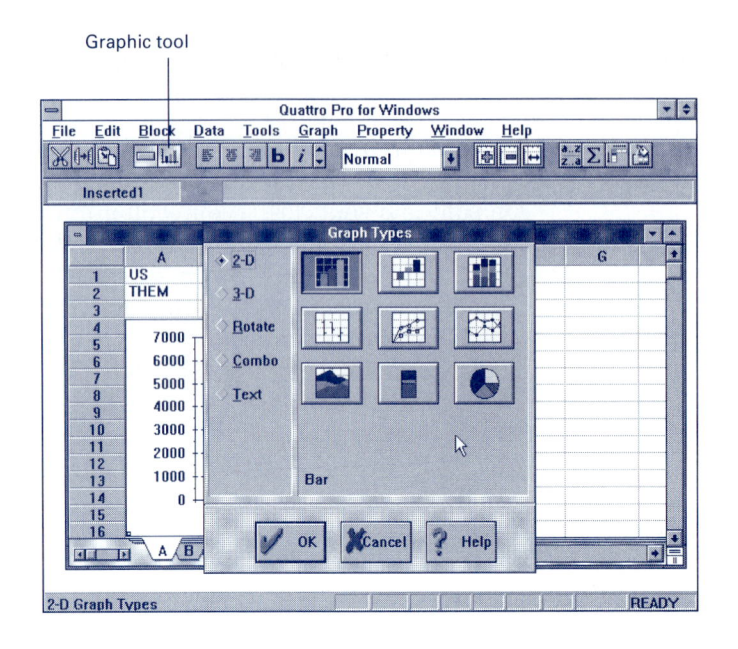

> **CAUTION:** In order for you to choose Graph!Type, the graph must be selected. Otherwise Type will be dimmed out on the Graph menu. You can tell a graph is selected because it will appear to have handles, eight small boxes along its frame. If when you click on Graph from the menu bar, Type is dimmed out, click on the graph to select it. Then click on Graph!Type.

2. Click on the pie chart, then on the OK button. The graph type will change to a pie chart and will look like Figure 7-2.

This graph really says it all. You don't need to add any other information. A graph that is part of a spreadsheet page in this way is called a **floating graph.** It is saved as a section of the page. It can be selected, moved, copied, pasted, and deleted like a cell block. To select a floating graph, click on it with the mouse. Then use the techniques you learned when working with cell blocks to move, copy, paste, or delete the graph.

PRINTING A FLOATING GRAPH

If you want to see the graph on paper, print out the notebook page.

1. Move to A1.

Figure 7-2
A pie chart

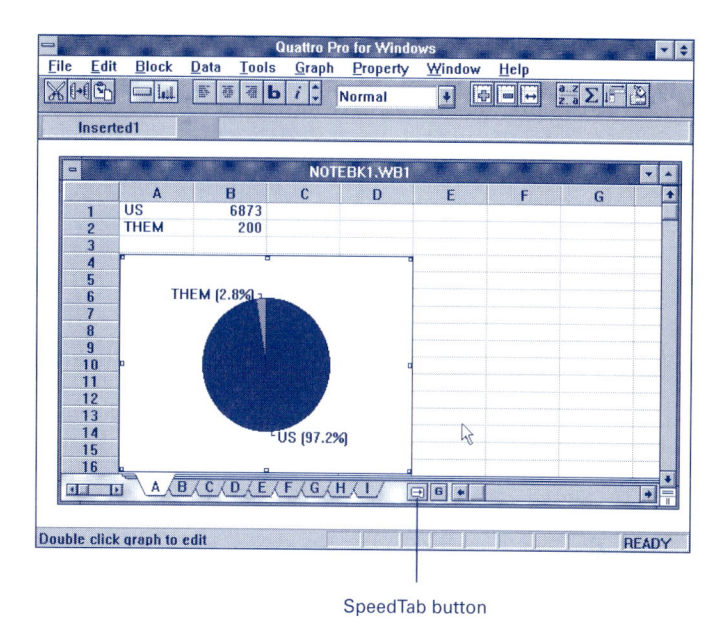

SpeedTab button

2. Select File | Print. Quattro Pro for Windows has selected the block A1..E16, which includes your new graph.

3. Click on the Print button. The notebook page, including the graph, will be printed.

Quattro Pro for Windows keeps track of all the graphs you create on the Graphs page, which is the last page of the notebook. To see the Graphs page:

1. Click on the SpeedTab button. In the upper left corner of the Graphs page you will see an icon for the graph. It is labeled "Graph1" (you will learn how to rename graphs later in the lesson).

2. Click on the SpeedTab button again to return to page A.

3. Save the notebook with the name CHART.WB1.

> **CAUTION:** *If you exit Quattro Pro for Windows without saving the notebook, the graph will be lost as well. Always be sure to save the notebook after creating a graph, if you want to keep it.*

You have finished with the CHART notebook and are ready to work with another one.

4. Select File | Close. CHART.WB1 will be removed from the screen.

CREATING A GRAPH USING THE GRAPH MENU

The Graph tool is very useful for simple graphs, but for more complicated ones, Quattro Pro for Windows provides the commands on the Graph menu and the Object Inspector menus. The procedure in creating a graph is to first decide what information you wish to graph and make sure that it is displayed correctly in the notebook. Then specify the blocks of data, or **series,** used to create the graph. The block used to define the values on the X-axis is called the **X-axis series;** the blocks used to define the values on the Y-axis are called the **Y-axis series.** You can define one X-axis series and up to six Y-axis series. You can include titles to identify the series. Like floating graphs, these can be saved with the notebook so that you have a permanent copy.

Specifying Series

Suppose that the report for your boss involves creating a graph of the book prices you entered in the BOOK notebook. You are interested in three different kinds of graphs: a display of titles and prices, the relationship between price and unit sales, and the relationship between price and total sales. A bar graph will display titles and prices most clearly; line graphs will present the relationships among series most effectively.

1. Open BOOK.WB1.
2. Move to A1 if you are not there already.
3. To create a new graph, select Graph | New. The Graph New dialog box is displayed (refer to Figure 7-3).

This menu allows you to specify the series for the graph. You can specify one X-series and up to six Y-series. For the first graph, you would like to display the book titles with their prices. The titles would make up the X-axis series; the prices would be the first Y-axis series. Follow these steps to specify series:

1. You will use Point mode to specify series. In Graph dialog boxes, you enter Point mode by clicking *once* on the button next to the edit field. To specify the X-series:

    a. Click once on the X-Axis button.

    b. Select the book titles, cells B4..B13.

    c. Click on the Maximize button on the Graph New title bar. You are returned to the Graph New dialog box.

2. To specify the Y-series:

    a. Click once on the "1st" button.

b. Select the prices, cells C4..C13.

c. Click on the Maximize button on the Graph New title bar. You are again returned to the Graph New dialog box (see Figure 7-3).

Figure 7-3
Selecting series using Point mode

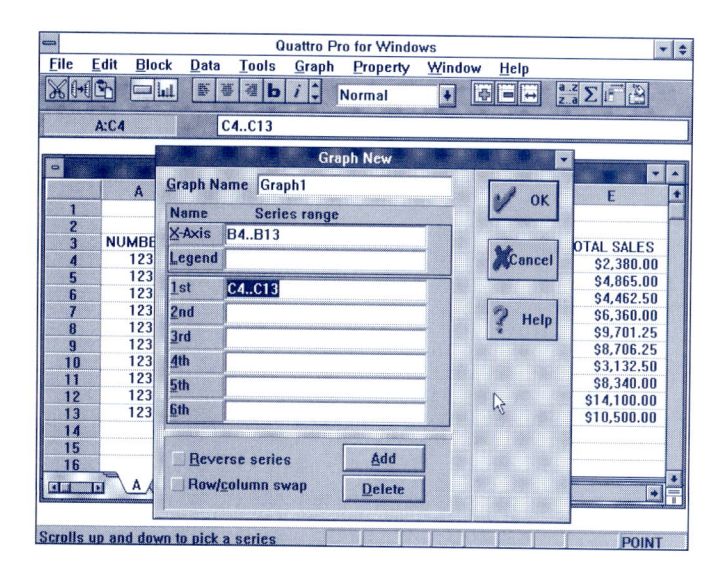

3. Click on OK. The graph is displayed. Notice that unlike the floating graph, this graph appears in a window, with the familiar title bar, Control menu button, and the Maximize and Minimize buttons.

Quattro Pro for Windows has created a graph, but it is not very elegant. There is only room to display a few of the titles on the X-axis. You could shorten the titles, but you really do want to display the full book titles on the graph. Perhaps the best idea would be to try another graph type.

Although a slightly different menu bar is displayed on the screen, you can still select Graph ¦ Type.

1. Select Graph ¦ Type.

Look at the list of graph types. How about trying Rotate?

2. Click on Rotate. The default selection is "Rotated 2-D Bar". Why not try it?

3. Click on the OK button to display a rotated, two-dimensional bar graph.

That's a little better. At least the book titles are now clearly displayed. But the bars are annoyingly truncated because the window is too small to display them properly.

4. Click on the Maximize button on the graph window to make more room for the graph. Now the graph is displayed properly (see Figure 7-4).

Figure 7-4
A graph displayed in a maximized window

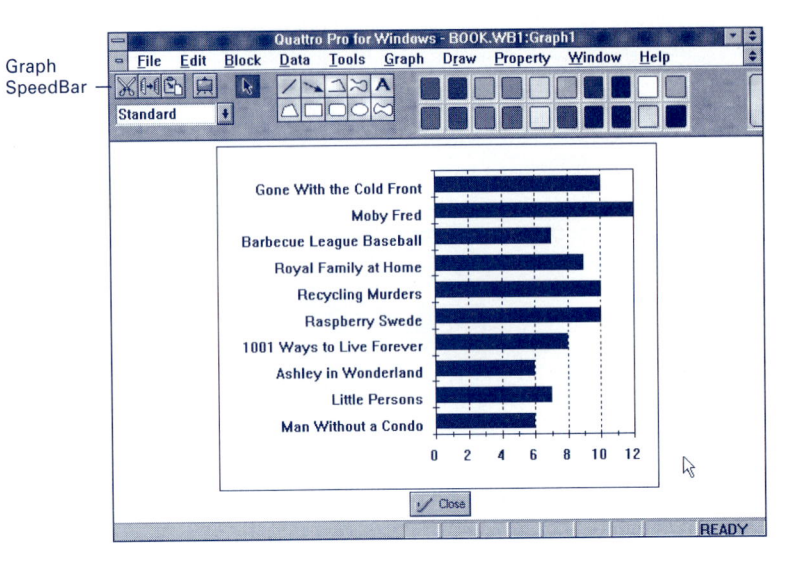

As you look at the graph, you may notice other features that could use some improvement. For one thing, the books are displayed in no particular order. As you think of it, you would like to display them in order of price. Nor is it clear that the numbers on the bottom are prices. And wouldn't a title be a useful addition?

To make these changes, first return to the notebook.

5. Click on the Close button.

Editing Series

The simplest way to organize the books by price is to sort them in that order. You learned how to do that in the last lesson.

1. Select the block to be sorted, A4..E13.

2. Select Data ¦ Sort.

3. You already know how to specify a sort key by typing the name of the field. You can also use Point mode and click on the field to use as the sort key.

    a. Double-click on the 1st edit field.

    b. Click on PRICE (cell C3).

    c. Click on the Maximize button on the Data Sort dialog box.

4. Click on OK. The data is sorted in order of price.

5. Click on A1 (or any other cell) to remove the highlight.

To see the difference this makes in the graph:

1. Select Graph | Edit. A dialog box is displayed listing graphs in this notebook. In this case, the only graph is Graph1.

2. Click on Graph1, then click on OK to view the graph.

As you can see, the graph has been changed to reflect the changes in the X-series.

Adding Text

To add a title to the graph:

1. Select Graph | Titles.

2. Type **BOOK PRICES**

You would also like to add a Y-axis title to identify the prices.

3. Click on the Y1-Axis Title edit field.

4. Type **Prices in dollars**

5. Click on the OK button. The graph is displayed with the changes you just made (see Figure 7-5).

Figure 7-5
The completed rotated bar graph

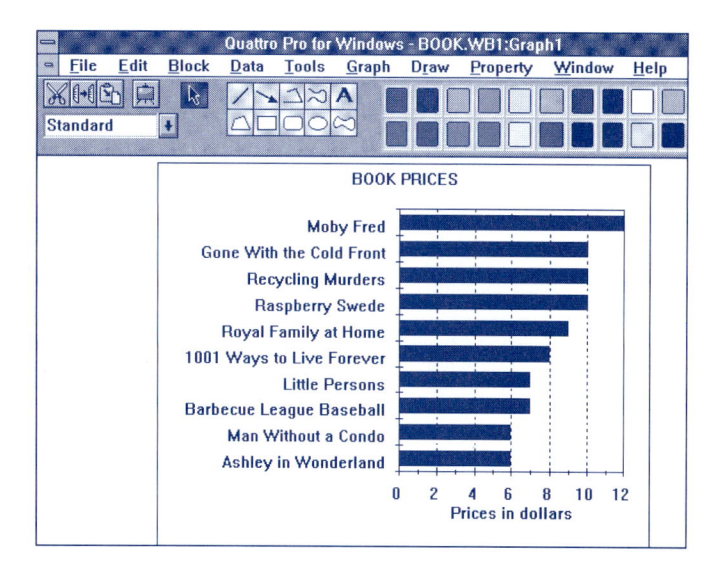

6. Click on the Close button to return to the notebook.

VIEWING A GRAPH FROM THE GRAPHS PAGE

Like the pie chart, this graph is saved on the Graphs page. To see it there:

1. Click on the SpeedTab button. The icon for Graph1 will be displayed.

Icons on the Graphs page behave like any other Windows icons. You can move them around the page and arrange them in any position you wish. You can also double-click on the graph icons to display the graph in a window, then close the window to display the graph as an icon again. To see how this works:

2. Double-click on the Graph1 icon. The graph is displayed in a window.

3. Click on the Close button to shrink Graph1 back to an icon. *Note:* You could also have selected Close after clicking on the Control menu button or by clicking on the Minimize button.

NAMING A GRAPH FROM THE GRAPHS PAGE

Wouldn't it be easier to identify the graph if you gave a more descriptive name? To give a graph a new name from the Graphs page, right-click on it. The Name dialog box appears. Type in the new name and press [Enter] or click on the OK button.

To rename Graph1 to Book Prices:

1. Right-click on Graph1.

2. Type **Book Prices** and press [Enter]. The graph name is changed to "Book Prices".

3. Click on the SpeedTab button to return to page A.

LINE GRAPHS

Next you will create a different kind of graph. Instead of developing a bar chart, suppose that you want to plot the relationship between book price and unit sales. If there were a relationship, it might affect future pricing of books. For that type of problem, a line graph would be useful. The PRICE values are used for the X-axis; the UNIT SALES are used for the Y-axis.

Follow these directions to create a line graph of book price and unit sales:

1. Select Graph | New to create a new graph.
2. To give the graph a new name, type **Book Sales** in the Graph Name edit field.
3. To specify the X-axis series, click on the X-Axis edit field and use Point mode to select the block C4..C13.
4. To specify the Y-axis series, click on the 1st edit field and use Point mode to select the block D4..D13.
5. Click on OK. The graph is displayed as a bar graph.
6. To change the graph type to line, select Graph | Type, click on the Line graph icon (refer to Figure 7-1), then click on OK.

To specify titles:

1. Select Graph | Titles.
2. Type **BOOK SALES** in the Main Title edit field.
3. Click on X-Axis Title and type **PRICES**
4. Click on Y1-Axis Title and type **UNIT SALES**
5. Click on OK. The graph is displayed.

The graph shows some relationship between price and unit sales; overall, as prices go up, so do sales. It seems likely that, within limits, sales are determined by a book's popularity, not just its price. The graph also shows that there is fluctuation within each price range and that the lowest priced book has unexpectedly high sales, as does one of the midpriced books. You can find out which are the unexpectedly high-selling books by returning to page A.

6. Click on Close to return to Page A. You can see that the lowest priced book is *Ashley in Wonderland,* and the midpriced book with high sales is *Barbecue League Baseball.*

Of course it would be much more convenient to be able to see, right on the graph, which book was which. For that you have to add **series labels.** You will see how to add them when you create the next graph.

ADDING SERIES LABELS USING OBJECT INSPECTOR MENUS

Plotting price against unit sales is useful, but you would gain additional information by creating a graph that plots price against total sales. Follow these steps to create it:

1. Select Graph | New.

2. To give the graph a new name, type **Total Sales** in the Graph Name edit field.

3. To specify the X-axis series, click on the X-Axis edit field and use Point mode to select the block C4..C13.

4. To specify the Y-axis series, click on the 1st edit field and use Point mode to select the block E4..E13.

5. Click on OK. The graph is displayed as a bar graph.

6. To change the graph type to line, select Graph | Type, click on the Line Graph icon, then click on OK.

7. To specify titles:

    a. Select Graph | Titles.

    b. Type **TOTAL SALES**

    c. Click on X-Axis Title and type **PRICES**

    d. Click on Y1-Axis Title and type **TOTAL SALES**

    e. Click on OK. The graph is displayed.

This graph suggests that the highest priced books generally make the most money for the store. If book sales really do depend more on popularity than price, maybe prices should be higher for the most popular books. On the other hand, consider *Barbecue League Baseball*. It has a comparatively low price, but it has the highest unit sales, giving it a high total sales value. If the price were raised, would it make even more money for the store? Or would sales drop? How about the other books in the $6.95 and $7.95 price range? Should the prices be raised, on the theory that the same number of people will continue to buy them? Or should prices be lowered, in the hope that unit sales will increase dramatically, thus increasing total sales?

Unfortunately Quattro Pro for Windows can't answer those questions for you. But it can help make the graph easier to read, by allowing you to add series labels, so that you can easily associate each book with its total sales. To add the labels, you will use Quattro Pro for Windows' Object Inspector menus. You can use this feature for graphs just as you can for cell blocks, by right-clicking on the part of the graph you want to enhance.

> **CAUTION:** Graphs are more complicated than cell blocks. You must be sure that you have positioned the mouse correctly in order to display the correct menu. If you accidentally display the wrong one, click on the Cancel button, reposition the mouse, and try again.

Follow these steps to display the book titles as labels:

1. Position the mouse pointer so that it points to the Y-series line.
2. Right-click. The Line Series Properties dialog box is displayed.
3. Use Point mode to specify the Label series, B4..B13 (see Figure 7-6).

Figure 7-6
Using Object Inspector menus to add series labels

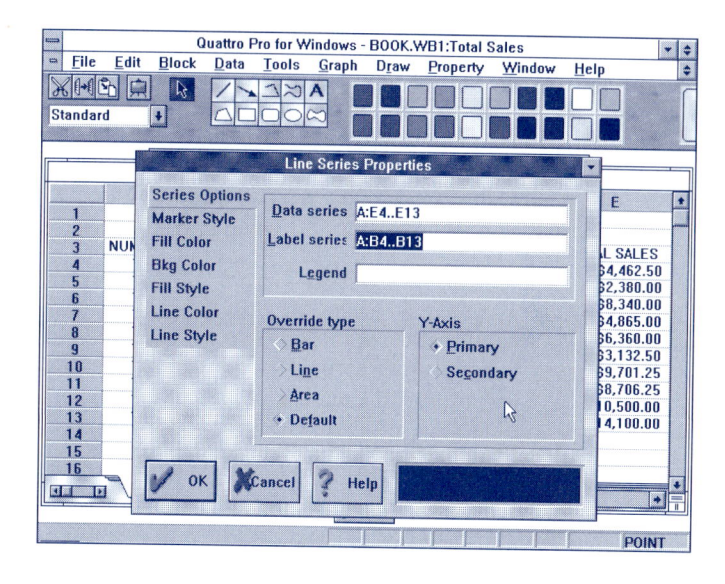

4. Click on the OK button. The Total Sales graph is displayed with series labels (see Figure 7-7).
5. Click on Close to return to page A when you have finished viewing the graph.

Figure 7-7
The Total Sales graph

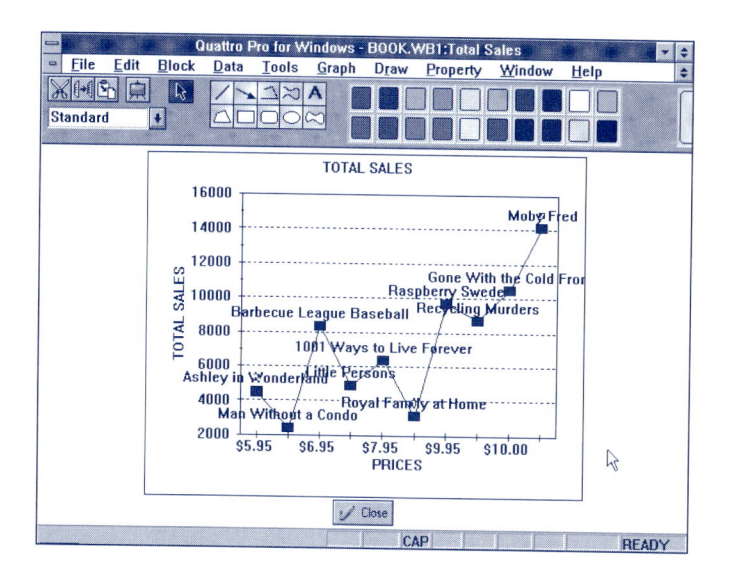

PRINTING A GRAPH

To print a graph quickly, you can simply select File | Print while displaying the graph in a window. The graph will be printed in portrait orientation, vertically on the page (you will learn more options for printing graphs in Lesson Nine). Follow these steps to print the Total Sales graph:

1. Select Graph | Edit, click on Total Sales to select it, and click on OK. The graph will be displayed again.
2. Select File | Print. The Graph Print dialog box appears.
3. Click on the Print button. In a few moments, the graph will be printed. *Note:* The graph may take some time to print, depending on the kind of printer you have.
4. Click on Close to return to page A.

Follow the same procedure for the other graphs you have created if you want to print them.

These graphs, like the pie chart you created earlier in the lesson, are stored on the Graphs page. To view the Graphs page of BOOK.WB1:

1. Click on the SpeedTab button. The Graphs page will be displayed with all three of the graphs you created using this notebook.
2. Click on the SpeedTab button again to return to page A.

You have now completed the graphs and will be able to present them to your boss on Monday without working all weekend. Before leaving Quattro Pro for Windows, make sure to save the notebook by selecting File | Save.

■ SUMMARY OF COMMANDS

Topic or Feature	Command or Reference	Menu	Page
Create a Floating Graph	Select data, then click on the Graph tool on the SpeedBar		103
Modify a Graph Type		Graph	Type	103
Select a Floating Graph	Click on it		104
Delete a Floating Graph	Click on it, then press Del		104
Move a Floating Graph	Drag it to the desired position		104

Topic or Feature	Command or Reference	Menu	Page
Print a Floating Graph		File ¦ Print	104
Create a New Graph		Graph ¦ New	106
Specify a Series for a New Graph		Graph ¦ New	106
Graph Titles		Graph ¦ Titles	109
Graph and Series Titles		Graph ¦ Titles	109
Edit an Existing Graph		Graph ¦ Edit	109
Name an Exisiting Graph	Right-click on the graph icon on the Graphs page	Object Inspector menus, from the graph icon on the Graphs page	110
View a Graph from the Graphs Page	Double-click on the graph icon		110
Restore a Graph to an Icon on the Graphs Page	Click on the Close button or the Minimize button	Control menu/ Close	110
Series Labels	Right-click on the graph series, then enter a block for labels	Object Inspector menus, from the graph series	111
Print a Graph		File ¦ Print	114
Save a Graph	Save the notebook	File ¦ Save	114

■ REVIEW QUESTIONS

1. What is the procedure for creating a floating graph?
2. What are the advantages of creating a floating graph?
3. What are the advantages of using the Graph menu?
4. How can you change the graph type?
5. What is a series?

First Look at Quattro Pro for Windows

6. List three graph types you have used and give an example of when to **use** each.

7. How many series can you specify for the Y-axis of a graph?

8. How many series can you specify for the X-axis of a graph?

9. What must you be careful of when using Object Inspector menus with graphs?

10. What happens to the current graph if you exit Quattro Pro for Windows without saving changes to the notebook?

■ HANDS-ON EXERCISES

Exercise 7-1 This exercise builds on Lesson Five, Exercise 5-1. Using CARS1.WB1, create a rotated bar graph plotting car make against price.

1. Define the list of car makes as the X-axis.
2. Define the prices as the Y-axis.
3. Add a graph title and series titles.
4. Add the list of models as series labels.
5. Save the graph with a descriptive name.
6. Print the graph.

Exercise 7-2 This exercise builds on Lesson Six, Exercise 6-2. One of your colleagues criticizes your limiting the price of the printers you are considering to under $1700. She argues that there is a relationship between price and quality: The higher the price, the better the printer. You aren't sure how she is defining "quality." But you can easily check whether there is a relationship between price and speed.

1. Create a graph plotting price against speed. Use your spreadsheet and graph skills to make the graph as clear as possible. Is there a relationship?
2. Save the graph and the notebook.

Exercise 7-3 1. Create a notebook using the following data on stocks, first-week prices, and second-week prices. Use the skills you have acquired to make the notebook as clear as possible.

Apple	44.13	44.50
AST Research	12.75	12.50

Chips & Technologies	4.50	4.63
Compaq	28.75	29.00
Conner Peripherals	20.38	19.50
DEC	37.50	35.25
Dell	23.13	25.63
Everex Systems	2.25	2.38
IBM	88.38	86.63
Intel	57.75	56.00
Sun Microsystems	25.38	26.13

2. Create a graph of these companies and stock prices. Use your graphing skills to make the graph as clear as possible. *Hint:* Each week's prices should be a separate series.

3. Assuming that the changes in price from week 1 to week 2 represent a trend, calculate the price of each stock at week 3. Then display those prices on your graph.

4. Save the graph.

5. Save the notebook with the name STOCK.WB1.

LESSON EIGHT

Working with Multiple-Page Notebooks

OBJECTIVES

At the end of this lesson, you will be able to:

- Move a block between pages.
- Change page names.
- Split the screen into two windows.
- Move between and within windows.
- Resize windows.
- Use File | Retrieve.
- Use drag and drop to move blocks.
- Use absolute cell references in multiple-page notebooks.
- Define a group of pages.
- Define noncontiguous blocks.
- Use SpeedBar buttons with grouped pages.
- Add cell contents across grouped pages.

So far you have been working with spreadsheet notebooks of only one page. But there might be reasons for working with more than one. Suppose, for instance, that you are a highly paid computer consultant and the notebook you developed in Lessons Two and Three contained the travel expenses incurred while working for one client. You have many more clients, each requiring a separate spreadsheet. How can you keep track of your total travel expenses? Or suppose that, in addition to your vacation paradise, you want to buy an airplane and a yacht to get there. The information on monthly payments for each purchase is on a separate spreadsheet. How can you find out what your total monthly payments will be? Or suppose that instead of managing just one bookstore you manage five of them and keep the inventory for each on a separate page. How can you combine the information to make intelligent marketing decisions?

You could put all the information onto one huge page. But you can only see one screen at a time, and you may lose track of which cells you used to store some vital information. Besides, printing out such a huge spreadsheet would be very awkward, even with the printing techniques you will learn in Lesson Nine. For those reasons, Quattro Pro for Windows allows you to create spreadsheet notebooks with multiple pages.

You will start off by dividing the Vacation Paradise notebook into two separate pages.

1. Open VACATION.WB1.
2. Move to A1 if you are not there already.

MOVING A BLOCK BETWEEN PAGES

This notebook really consists of two separate parts. The top part lists vacation homes and their prices, with information about the number of properties and the maximum and minimum price. The bottom part lists the monthly payments on a loan covering the price of the property. What you want to do now is move the bottom part to page B. You can use the Cut and Paste buttons to move information between pages in the same way you used them to move cell contents within pages. Follow these steps to move the monthly payments to page B:

1. Move to page B by clicking on its tab.
2. Move to B1.
3. Type **VACATION PARADISE, PAGE TWO** and press ⌈Enter⌋
4. Move back to page A by clicking on its tab.
5. Move to A25 and select all the information about monthly payments (block A25..D43).
6. Click on the Cut button.
7. Move to page B, cell A3.
8. Click on the Paste button. The information is moved to page B (see Figure 8-1).

But the data is impossible to read this way! Quattro Pro for Windows has moved the cell contents but not the cell widths. Widen the columns to display the information.

1. Select columns A through D by dragging the mouse.
2. Click on the Fit button. The column widths are automatically adjusted.
3. Click on any cell to remove the highlight from the selected columns.

Move to A8 and look at the input line to see what Quattro Pro for Windows has done. The input line reads "+A:A5". You originally entered a link in this cell to cell A5 on page A by typing +A5; Quattro Pro for Windows supplied

Figure 8-1
Moving data between notebook pages

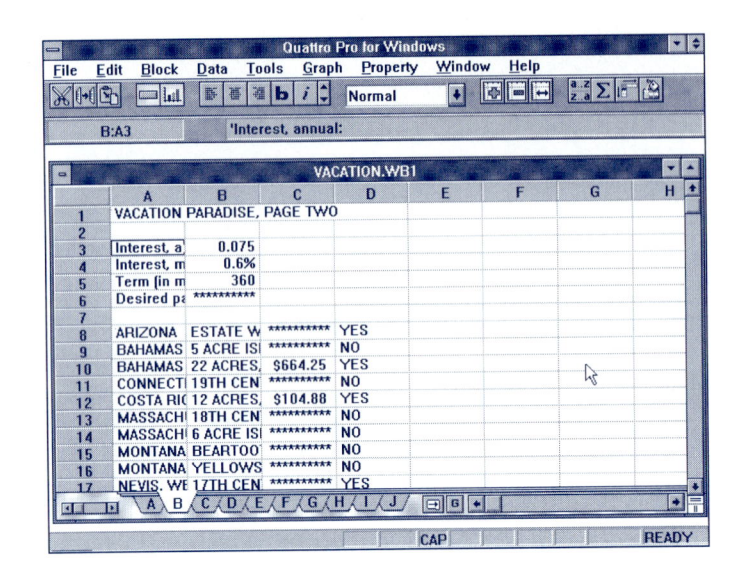

the "A:". Even though you have moved the link to page B, the program assumed that you still wanted a link to cell A5 on page A. If you move to B8, you will see that the same thing has happened: The input line reads "+A:B5", telling you that the link to cell B5 on page A has been maintained.

Now move to C8 and look at the input line. The input line reads "@PMT(A:C5,$B:$B$4,$B:$B$5)". Note that the original formula was "@PMT(A:C5,$A:$B$26,$A:$B$27)". But when you moved the contents of cells B26 and B27 from page A to cells B4 and B5 on page B, Quattro Pro for Windows assumed that you wanted to adjust all the formulas that were linked to those cells so that those links were maintained.

Changing Page Names

Since you have divided the notebook information into two pages, you will find it useful to give each page a descriptive name. That way you can easily tell what information it contains. You give each page a name with Object Inspector menus by positioning the mouse pointer on the page tab and right-clicking.

Follow the steps below to give page A the name "Prices" and page B the name "Monthly_Payment".

NOTE: Page names cannot contain spaces. If you want to use more than one word as a page name, type a one-character line (_) where the space would go, as in Monthly_Payment.

1. Click on the tab for page A to make that the active page.

2. Right-click on the tab. A dialog box is displayed with the pointer set up at the Page Name edit field.

3. Type **Prices** (see Figure 8-2).

Figure 8-2
Changing page names using Object Inspector menus

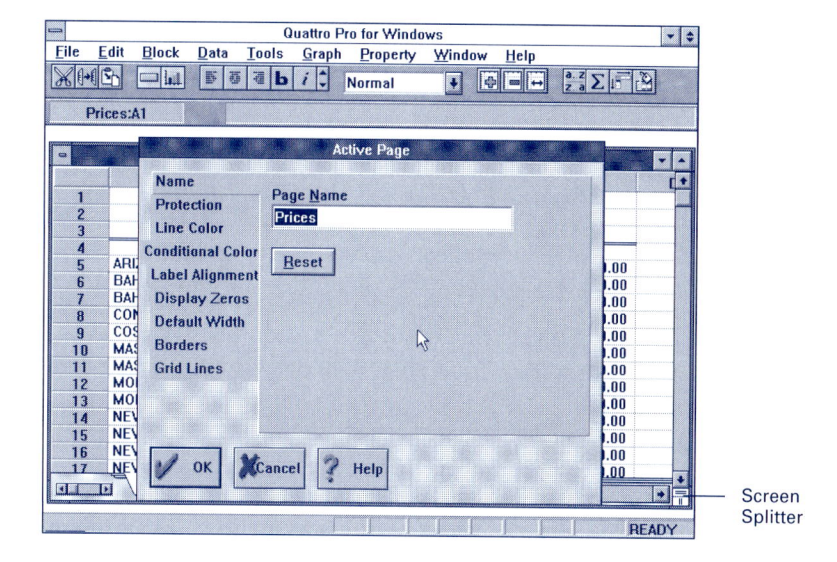

4. Press Enter. The tab now displays the name "Prices".

5. Click on the tab for page B to make that the active page.

6. Right-click on the tab. Type **Monthly_Payment** and press Enter. The tab now displays the name "Monthly_Payment".

7. Click on the Prices tab to return to the first page.

As you can see, it is extremely useful to be able to give pages descriptive names. It can help you find the information you need very easily, even if your notebook consists of many pages. Once you have renamed the pages, all the cell addresses are updated to reflect the new page names. To see this, move around the page and look at the box to the left of the input line.

1. Move to the title, cell B1. Instead of "A:B1", the box next to the input line reads "Prices:B1".

2. Move to A20. The box next to the input line reads "Prices:A20".

Page names are also changed in formulas.

3. Move to Monthly_Payment by clicking on the tab, then to cell C8. The formula now reads "@PMT(Prices:C5,$Monthly_Payment:$B$4, $Monthly_Payment:$B$5)", instead of "@PMT(A:C5,$B:$B$4,$B:$B$5)".

4. Move to A1. Then click on Prices and move to A1.

SPLITTING THE SCREEN INTO TWO WINDOWS

Another useful technique for working with more than one page at a time is splitting the screen into two windows, each of which displays a different page. Since it is a frequently used technique, Quattro Pro for Windows provides a shortcut, the **Screen Splitter,** in the bottom right corner of the notebook (refer to Figure 8-2). Click on the top part of the Screen Splitter to divide the screen horizontally into two **windows,** one above the other. Click on the bottom part of the Screen Splitter to divide the screen vertically into two side-by-side windows.

Follow these steps to divide the screen into two windows, the top displaying Prices and the bottom displaying Monthly_Payment:

1. Position the mouse on the top part of the Screen Splitter. The usual mouse arrow is replaced by a two-headed arrow with a horizontal bar.

> *CAUTION: If you position the mouse on the bottom part of the Screen Splitter, the mouse arrow will be replaced by a two-headed arrow with a vertical bar. Move the mouse up slowly until it changes to the arrow with the horizontal bar.*

2. Position the mouse on the top part of the Screen Splitter and press the left mouse button. A dotted horizontal line appears.

3. Drag the line until it is between rows 9 and 10, just under the information for Costa Rica. Then release the mouse button. The screen is split into two windows, each displaying part of the Prices page.

4. Click on the Monthly_Payment tab in the lower window. The Monthly_Payment page is displayed (see Figure 8-3).

Moving Between and Within Windows

To move between windows, click on any part of the window you wish to use. By clicking on the page tab in the bottom window, you moved to that window. To move back to the top window, click on any cell in it.

1. Click on A1 in Prices.

2. Click on B5 in Monthly_Payment to move to that page.

Once you are in a window, you can use the keyboard and mouse to move around in the same way as you would if there were only one window displayed. You can also use the SpeedBar or menu bar to edit the notebook page

Figure 8-3
Splitting the screen into two windows

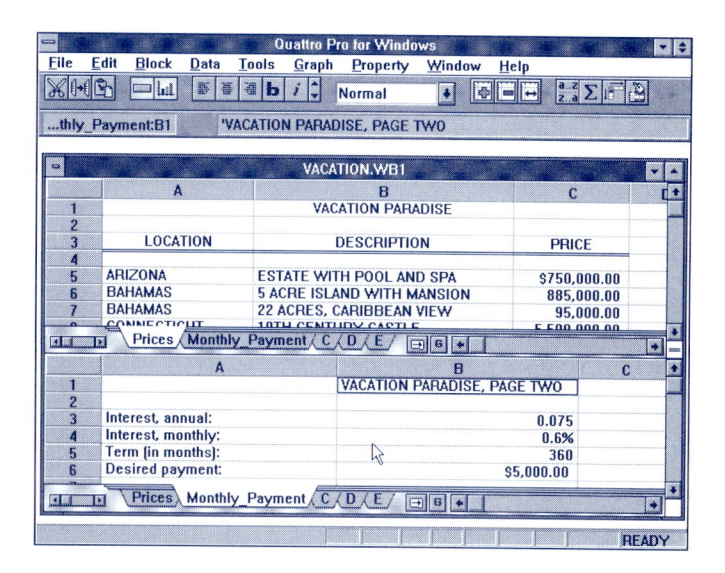

without affecting the other window. Of course any changes you make to cells in one window that are referenced by cells in the other window will affect the second window.

Follow these steps to practice working with windows:

1. Click on A5 in Prices.
2. Press ↓ six times so that the Arizona property is at the top of the screen.
3. Click on A6 in Monthly_Payment.
4. Press ↓ seven times so that the Arizona property is at the top of the screen.

The two pages should be lined up so that each displays the list of properties. Next you will change the price of the Arizona property in the top window and see how it changes the monthly payments in the bottom window.

5. Move to C5 in Prices by clicking on it.
6. Edit the value to read 750000 and press (Enter). As you can see, Quattro Pro for Windows has automatically updated the value in C8 in Monthly_Payment to $5244.11. D8 in Monthly_Payment has also been updated to "NO", because the monthly payments now exceed the desired payment of $5000 (see Figure 8-4).

Resizing Windows

Use the Screen Splitter to resize windows. Position the mouse pointer on the Screen Splitter, now in the top window (refer to Figure 8-4). Press the left

Figure 8-4
Viewing changes in linked cell references

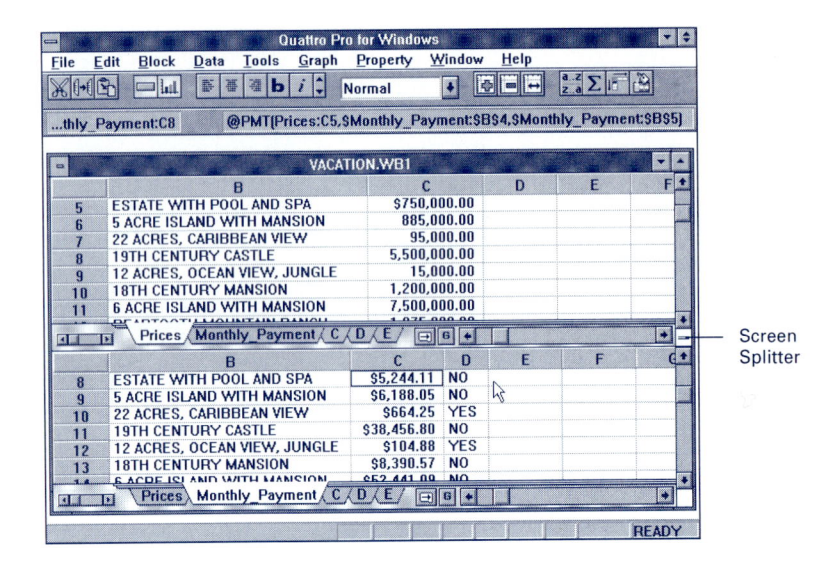

[Screenshot of Quattro Pro for Windows showing VACATION.WB1 with a split screen view. Upper pane shows Prices page with property listings (Estate with Pool and Spa $750,000.00, 5 Acre Island with Mansion $885,000.00, 22 Acres Caribbean View $95,000.00, 19th Century Castle $5,500,000.00, 12 Acres Ocean View Jungle $15,000.00, 18th Century Mansion $1,200,000.00, 6 Acre Island with Mansion $7,500,000.00). Lower pane shows Monthly Payment calculations ($5,244.11 NO, $6,188.05 NO, $664.25 YES, $38,456.80 NO, $104.88 YES, $8,390.57 NO). Screen Splitter label points to the divider.]

mouse button and drag the horizontal dotted line until the top window is the desired size. The bottom window will automatically adjust to fit the remainder of the screen. To return to a single-window view, drag the horizontal dotted line all the way to the bottom of the screen.

To reunite the split screen and return to a single window:

1. Position the mouse pointer on the Screen Splitter and press the left mouse button. The horizontal dotted line will appear.

2. Drag the line to the bottom of the screen and release the mouse button. Only the Prices page is displayed.

You have finished with VACATION.WB1 for now. Select File ¦ Save to save it. You will use the notebook EXPENSES.WB1 to explore other advantages to multiple pages.

USING FILE ¦ RETRIEVE

At this point, you would like to leave VACATION.WB1 and display EXPENSES.WB1. You could do this by using File ¦ Close to close VACATION.WB1 and File ¦ Open to open EXPENSES.WB1. However, Quattro Pro for Windows provides a command, File ¦ Retrieve, that does both at once.

1. Select File ¦ Retrieve. You are prompted for a file, as you are when using the File ¦ Open command.

2. Select EXPENSES.WB1. VACATION.WB1 will be closed and EXPENSES.WB1 will be displayed on the screen.

DIVIDING A NOTEBOOK INTO MULTIPLE PAGES

When you originally set up this notebook, you put all the information about travel expenses on one page. But when you have several sets of information all arranged in the same way, as in this notebook, there are advantages to dividing it among several pages. Suppose that you have decided that the information would be easier to read if each trip were placed on a separate page, with the total expenses listed on all pages. You could also have a separate "Total" page to add up the cost of hotels, meals, airfares, and taxis. Quattro Pro for Windows makes it simple to carry out this rearrangement by allowing you to **group** the pages together, so that editing techniques like Paste and Fit can be carried out across all of them at once. You can also add cells across pages as well as within them to quickly calculate totals on the Total page.

To see how these operations work, you will first redesign the notebook. You will rename page A "San_Francisco", page B "Paris", page C "Tokyo", and page D "Total". Then you will move the information on Paris expenses to the Paris page and the information on Tokyo expenses to the Tokyo page. Finally you will move the Total Expenses information closer to the top of the page and add absolute cell references to it. Follow these steps to change page names:

1. Right-click on tab A. Type **San_Francisco** and press [Enter]
2. Right-click on tab B. Type **Paris** and press [Enter]
3. Right-click on tab C. Type **Tokyo** and press [Enter]
4. Right-click on tab D. Type **Total** and press [Enter]

Next, move the information to the appropriate page.

1. Move to B9 on the San_Francisco page.
2. Select cells B9..E13 and click on the Cut button.
3. Move to B3 on the Paris page and click on the Paste button.
4. Select column E and click on the Fit button to widen the column.
5. Move to B15 on the San_Francisco page, select B15..E19, and click on the Cut button.
6. Move to B3 on the Tokyo page and click on the Paste button.
7. Select columns D and E and click on the Fit button.

Since you have moved the information on travel expenses, you no longer need the foreign exchange rates on the San_Francisco page. The information on francs should be on the Paris page; the information on yen should be on the Tokyo page. Follow these steps to move it:

1. Move to F3 on San_Francisco. Select F3..G3 and click on the Cut button.
2. Move to F3 on Paris and click on the Paste button. The information on francs will be copied.
3. Move to F4 on San_Francisco. Select F4..G4 and click on the Cut button.
4. Move to F3 on Tokyo and click on the Paste button. The information on yen will be copied.

Using Drag and Drop to Move Blocks

The final step is to move the Total Expenses information from B21..E21 to just below the San Francisco expenses and make the cell references absolute. You will do the former using the drag and drop technique you learned in Lesson Three. In that lesson, you used it to *copy* blocks of cells. The technique for *moving* cells requires less effort.

1. Move to B21 on the San_Francisco page.
2. Select B21..E21.
3. Position the mouse anywhere on the block and press the left mouse button. The arrow on the block will turn into a small hand, and the outline of the block will be highlighted.
4. Drag the block outline until it is positioned to cover cells B9..E9, then release the left mouse button. The total expenses information has been moved.

Take a look at the information on the San_Francisco page. In addition to the San Francisco expenses, it includes the title of the notebook, "Travel Expenses", and the total expenses. It would be useful to include this information on all the pages, so that you could easily find the title and total expenses no matter which page is displayed. You could copy each piece of information separately to each page using the techniques you already know. But Quattro Pro for Windows has two features, **grouped pages** and **noncontiguous blocks,** that make copying much easier.

Absolute Cell References with Multiple-Page Notebooks

Before copying the information, though, you will need to modify the function for Total Expenses in E9, because it was originally written with relative cell references. That was fine as long as all the information was on the same page. Now, however, the information is spread out over three pages.

1. Move to E9 in San_Francisco and look at the function on the input line. It reads "@SUM(San_Francisco..Tokyo:D3..D6)", letting you know that

Quattro Pro for Windows is adding the values in block D3..D6 on all pages from San_Francisco through Tokyo. What happens if you copy it to the next page?

2. To find out, click the Copy button, move to E9 in Paris, and click on the Paste button. The total expenses seem to have decreased: E9 in Paris now reads $3943.72.

3. To see why, look at the input line of E9 in Paris. It reads "@SUM(Paris..Total:D3..D6)", indicating that it is now adding all the values in block D3..D6 on pages Paris through Total. That is, it has maintained the same position relative to the *pages,* as well as to the cells. The values from the San_Francisco page have been left out, so the total is incorrect.

4. Press [Del] to delete the function, since you have no need for an incorrect formula in your notebook.

The solution is to add absolute cell references to the function in E9 of San_Francisco. Then it will always refer to the correct cells.

1. Move to E9 in San_Francisco.

2. Press [F2] to edit the cell and then press [F4] in order to make the cell references absolute. The function now reads "@SUM($San_Francisco ..$Tokyo:$D$3..$D$6)".

3. Press [Enter]

DEFINING A GROUP OF PAGES

You are now ready to define a *group* of pages to work with. When pages are grouped, changes made to one affect all the others. You first define a group with the Tools ǀ Group command. Then use the **Group button** (refer to Figure 8-5) at the bottom of the notebook to turn Group mode on and off. You can define any number of pages as a group, and you can have many different groups within each notebook. However, no page can be in more than one group at a time.

To define all the pages from San_Francisco through Total as one group:

1. Click on the tab for the first page of the group (in this case, San_Francisco).

2. Hold down the [Shift] key with one hand and click on the tab for the last page of the group (in this case, Total). A dark line appears underneath the tabs of the grouped pages.

3. Select Tools ǀ Define Group. A dialog box appears with edit fields for the group name, first page, and last page. Since you have already specified a first and last page, the names are already filled in to the edit boxes (again, see Figure 8-5). *Note:* You could have selected Tools ǀ Define Group first and typed in the name of the pages yourself.

4. Type **Expenses** in the Group Name edit field. Your screen should look like Figure 8-5.

Figure 8-5
Defining grouped pages

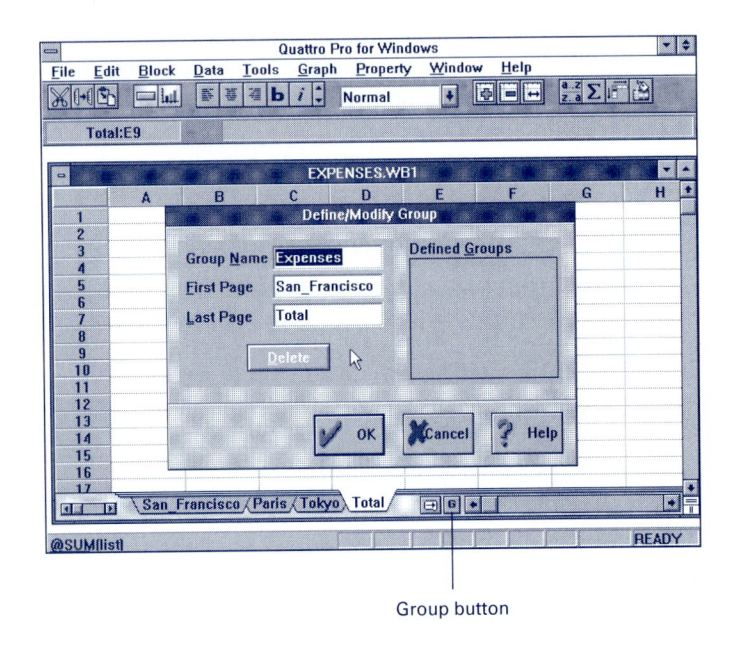

Group button

5. Press [Enter]. The group Expenses is defined as consisting of pages San_Francisco, Paris, Tokyo, and Total.

You turn on Group mode whenever you want to carry out an operation across all pages at once. Turn it off when you want to work with one page at a time.

1. Press the Group button to turn on Group mode. A line appears underneath the page tabs.

2. Press the Group button again to turn off Group mode for now.

DEFINING NONCONTIGUOUS BLOCKS

What you would like to do next is copy the notebook title and total expenses from the San_Francisco page to all the other pages. Instead of copying each block separately, you can do it all at once by defining a *noncontiguous block*—

which is just what it sounds like: a set of cells that do not necessarily touch each other. You define it by holding down Ctrl with one hand while dragging the mouse to select each set of cells in turn. To define the noncontiguous block to copy from San_Francisco:

1. Move to A1 in San_Francisco.
2. Hold down Ctrl while doing the following:

    a. Drag the mouse to select A1..B1.

    b. Move the mouse to B9 and drag it to select B9..E9.

3. Release Ctrl. The two separate blocks should be highlighted, indicating that they have been selected.

> **CAUTION:** *If you make a mistake while selecting the blocks, release* Ctrl *and click on A1 to begin again. Remember to drag the mouse slowly to make sure you select the correct cells.*

4. Click on the Copy button to copy the block.

USING SPEEDBAR BUTTONS WITH GROUPED PAGES

The next step is to paste the block in the other three pages. This requires you to turn on Group mode, then paste the block only once. Quattro Pro for Windows will automatically paste it in the other pages.

1. Click on the Group button to enter Group mode.
2. Click on A1 in Total and click on the Paste button. The block is copied to the Total page.

As you can see, although the block has been copied correctly, column E on the Total page is too narrow to display the value for total expenses.

3. Select column E.
4. Click on the Fit button to widen the column and display the total expenses.
5. Move to the Tokyo and Paris pages to verify that the block has been copied.
6. Move back to A1 in San_Francisco.
7. Click on the Group button to turn off Group mode for now.

> **CAUTION:** Always turn off Group mode when you are finished with the operation that required it. Otherwise you may make a mistake and change all the pages in a group when you only meant to change one page!

ADDING CELL CONTENTS ACROSS GROUPED PAGES

The final task to complete the Travel Expenses notebook is to add up the totals for hotels, meals, airfares, and taxis and place them on the Total page. Begin by copying the labels from the San_Francisco page to Total.

1. Select C3..C6 and click on Copy.

2. Move to C3 in Total and click on Paste. The labels are copied.

3. To remove the line from C6 in Total, right-click on C6, select Line Drawing, click on the No Line button under Line Types, on the bottom line under Line Segments, and on OK.

Now you will use the SpeedSum button to add cells D3..D6 across all the pages and place the totals in cells D3..D6 on Total. That is, you want Quattro Pro for Windows to add the value in San_Francisco:D3+Paris:D3+Tokyo:D3 and place the sum in Total:D3, then do the same for all the values in D4 and D5 across the three pages. The procedure is to select the cells, click on the Group button to enter Group mode, and click on SpeedSum to get the totals. For this to work, all the cells you want to add must be in the same position on each page, and the last page of the group must have blank cells in that position.

1. Move to D3 in San_Francisco and select cells D3..D6.

2. Click on the Group button to enter Group mode.

3. Click on SpeedSum.

4. Move to the Total page to verify that the values have been added.

Follow the same procedure to add the values in E7 across all pages.

1. Move to E7 in San_Francisco and select it by clicking on it.

2. You are still in Group mode, so this time just click on SpeedSum.

3. Click on the Group button to turn off Group mode.

4. Move to Total and use the technique you learned for selecting noncontiguous blocks to format the values D3..D6 and E7 for Currency, 2 decimal places.

   a. While holding down Ctrl, select D3..D6 and E9.

   b. Right-click on the block to bring up the Object Inspector menu and select Currency format, 2 decimal places.

5. Select column D and click on the Fit button to widen the column.

6. Return to A1 in San_Francisco.

As you have learned, using multiple pages can make notebooks easier to read as well as make notebook operations easier to carry out. You have completed the EXPENSES.WB1 notebook. Select File ǀ Save to save your changes and then exit Quattro Pro for Windows.

■ SUMMARY OF COMMANDS

Topic or Feature	Command or Reference	Menu	Page
Move a Block Between Pages	Cut and Paste buttons on the SpeedBar	Block ǀ Move	119
Page Names	Right-click on the page tab	Object Inspector menus, from the page tab	120
Split the Screen into Two Windows	Drag the Screen Splitter		122
Move Between Windows	Click on any cell in a window to make it the active window		122
Close the Active Notebook and Open an Existing Notebook		File ǀ Retrieve	124
Move a Block	Drag the block to a new location	Block ǀ Move	126
Copy a Block Between Pages	Copy and Paste buttons on the SpeedBar	Block ǀ Copy	126

Topic or Feature	Command or Reference	Menu	Page
Define a Group of Pages	Click on the first page of a group, hold down [Shift], then click on the last page of the group	Tools ¦ Define Group	127
Group Mode	Click on the Group button		128
Define Noncontiguous Blocks	Hold down [Ctrl] while selecting the blocks with the mouse		128
Paste Cell Contents to All Pages in a Group	Click on the Group button, then use the Paste button from the SpeedBar		129
Add Cell Contents Across Grouped Pages	Click on the Group button, then use SpeedSum from the SpeedBar		130

■ REVIEW QUESTIONS

1. What steps would you follow to move a block of cells to a new page in a notebook?

2. What steps would you follow to copy a block of cells to a new page in a notebook?

3. You wish to move the function @COUNT(A:B10..A:B25) from A:C10 to B:B1. What will the function in B:B1 be?

4. You wish to copy the function @COUNT(A:B10..A:B25) from A:C10 to B:B1. What will the function in B:B1 be?

5. You wish to copy the function @COUNT($A:$B$10..$A:$B$25) from A:C10 to B:B1. What will the function in B:B1 be?

6. What is the procedure for splitting the screen into two windows?

7. When is it useful to use File ¦ Retrieve rather than File ¦ Close?

8. How can you use drag and drop to move blocks? How can you use drag and drop to copy blocks?

9. What is the procedure for defining a group of pages?

10. How can you select a noncontiguous block?

11. How do you enter Group mode?

12. What is the advantage of Group mode?

■ HANDS-ON EXERCISES

Exercise 8-1 This exercise builds on the exercises in Lesson Two. If you created WOOL2.WB1, open it. If not, open WOOL1.WB1.

a. Edit the notebook so that each store's inventory is displayed on a separate page. Use the techniques discussed in this lesson to display the information as clearly as possible.

b. Give each page a name.

c. Create a Totals page for your total costs and prices.

d. Save the notebook with the changes.

Exercise 8-2 You have just been hired by a foundation that runs summer schools for gifted and talented teenagers. There are five summer schools offering a total of ten courses, but not all schools offer all the courses. Part of your job is to order textbooks, study guides, and lab equipment for each class. You must order the supplies through a central office and see that they are distributed to the correct summer school in the correct amounts. If you order too few, some students will go without textbooks or study guides; if you order too many, you are wasting scarce foundation funds. You therefore want to set up a notebook to keep track of enrollments in each class at each summer school, with a Totals page to let you know how many of each supply you must order.

Use the following list of summer school sites, classes, and enrollments in this notebook:

Harvard	Math	25
	Writing	25
	French	10
	Spanish	15
	Paleontology	17
	Archaeology	13
	German	22
	Biology	12
	Chemistry	15
	Physics	19

Princeton	Writing	46
	French	22
	Spanish	15
	German	30
Yale	Math	25
	Biology	25
	Chemistry	23
	Physics	28
Stanford	Writing	12
	Spanish	24
	Paleontology	8
	Archaeology	7
	Biology	21

a. Set up the notebook, using the skills you have learned in this text.

b. Create a Totals page to calculate the total amount of textbooks, study guides, and lab equipment you will have to order. Assume each student gets his or her own. You will need textbooks and study guides for all classes, but lab equipment only for science classes.

c. You need to keep track of the total number of students at each summer school to order general supplies like paper and exam books. Include totals for each summer school and for all summer schools in your notebook.

d. Save the notebook as SUPPLY.WB1.

LESSON NINE: Printing Notebooks and Graphs

OBJECTIVES

At the end of this lesson, you will be able to:
- Print a multiple-page notebook on one page.
- Add text for headers and footers.
- Center text on the printed page.
- Preview your work before printing it.
- Adjust margins.
- Change the font attributes of headers.
- Print from the Preview screen.
- Save print settings.
- Select a multiple-page print block.
- Print notebook pages separately.
- Modify the alignment of headers and footers and include the date and page number.
- Create headers from row and column labels.
- Print graphs from the Graphs page.
- Add headers and footers to graphs.

You already know how to print a page of a notebook quickly. This lesson will demonstrate how to print notebook pages and graphs using advanced features such as headers and footers, page numbers, and page breaks. It will also demonstrate printing graphs. Most of the features you will use are found on the File menu under Print, Print Preview, and Page Setup. You will print pages from the EXPENSES, VACATION, and BOOK notebooks; you will print graphs from the BOOK notebook.

PRINTING A MULTIPLE-PAGE NOTEBOOK ON ONE PAGE

As you learned in Lesson Four, the first time you try to print a notebook, Quattro Pro for Windows assumes you want to print all the information on the active page of that notebook. You could therefore print out each page of a notebook simply by making each one in turn the active page and selecting File ¦ Print. In most cases, though, you would prefer to print out the information in a more elegant form, either by printing it all on one page or by printing headers and footers on all pages.

For the first example, you will print all the pages in EXPENSES.WB1 on one page. You can do this very easily using Group mode.

1. Open EXPENSES.WB1 and move to A1 in San_Francisco, if you are not there already.

2. Click on the Group button to turn on Group mode.

3. Select cells A1..G9. You must select through G9 because you are selecting cells across all four pages and want to include the foreign currency information on the Paris and Tokyo pages.

4. Select File ¦ Print. The Print block edit field should read "Expenses:A1..G9", letting you know the block has been correctly selected.

5. Click on the Print button. The notebook will be printed.

You have printed all the information in the notebook, but it is not presented very elegantly. The titles "Travel Expenses" and "Total Expenses: $5,386.67" have been printed four times, since they appear once on each page. The columns don't line up properly, since they have different widths on each page. And wouldn't the whole page look better if the information were centered? Fortunately you can improve the appearance of the page by editing the notebook and by changing some of Quattro Pro for Windows' built-in print options.

The first step is to make the widths of columns B through G equal across all pages. You can do this very easily in Group mode by selecting columns and right-clicking to choose Column Width. All the columns on all four pages will automatically be affected by the width you choose.

1. Check to make sure that you are still in Group mode.

2. Right-click on column B, select a column width of 25, and press [Enter]

3. Select columns C through G, right-click, select a column width of 10 and press [Enter]. The column widths on all pages will be automatically adjusted.

Setting Headers and Footers

The next step is to set headers and footers. Instead of including "Travel Expenses" in cells A1..B1 and the information on total expenses in B9..E9, you will use File │ Page Setup to type in a header ("TRAVEL EXPENSES FOR BUSINESS TRIPS") and a new footer ("TOTAL EXPENSES: $5,386.67").

1. Select File │ Page Setup. A dialog box is displayed (refer to Figure 9-1).

2. Click on the Header edit field and type **TRAVEL EXPENSES FOR BUSINESS TRIPS**

3. Click on the Footer edit field and type **TOTAL EXPENSES: $5,386.67** (your screen should look like Figure 9-1).

Figure 9-1
Setting up a notebook to print

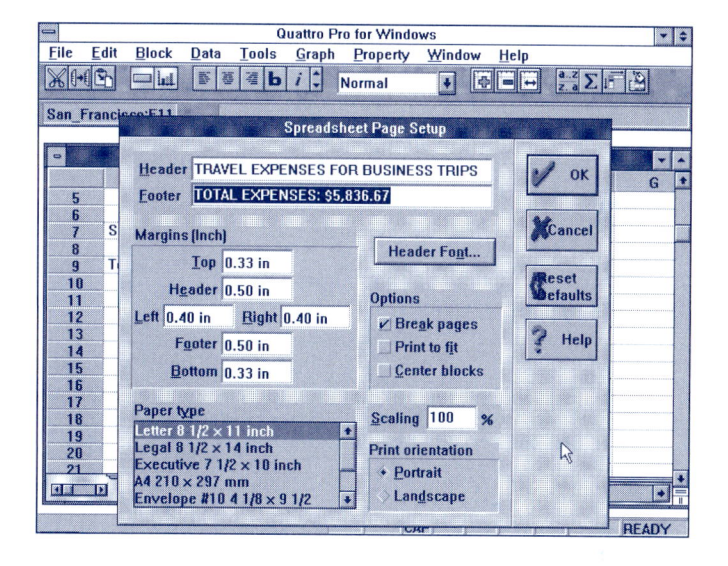

Centering Text on the Printed Page

This dialog box also allows you to choose whether you want to center the information on the page. Click on Center blocks (under Options) to center the information. A check will appear. To have the information left-justified, click on Center blocks again to remove the check.

1. To center the information on the page, click on Center blocks, under Options.

2. When done, click on OK to return to the notebook.

Having chosen a header and footer, you now have to select a new block to print, since you no longer want to include cells A1..B1 or B9..E9.

1. Select B3..G7.

2. Select File │ Print.

138 First Look at Quattro Pro for Windows

PREVIEWING BEFORE PRINTING

You could try printing the notebook to see what happens. But a better way of finding out how the printed notebook will look is to click on the Preview button. This will display the notebook in a special **Preview screen,** allowing you to see what the final printed version will look like. It also allows you to make changes to the notebook before printing it out.

1. To preview your work from the File Print dialog box, click on the Preview button. Your notebook will be displayed on the Preview screen (see Figure 9-2).

NOTE: You can also select Print Preview from the File menu. Clicking on the Preview button is useful, though, because Quattro Pro for Windows will return you to the Print dialog box when you are finished previewing your work.

Figure 9-2
Previewing the notebook before printing

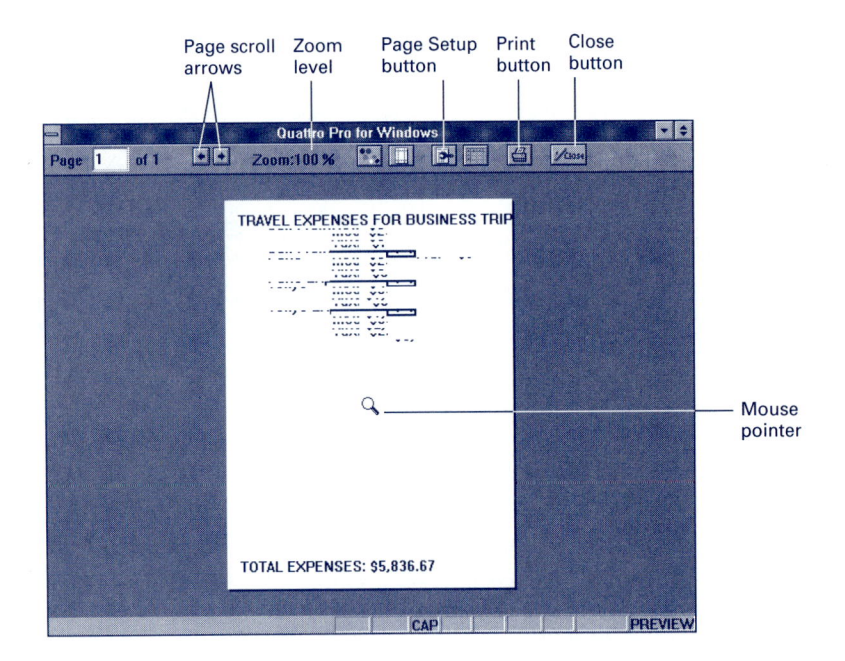

Take some time to explore the Preview screen. Just above the display area is the SpeedBar. The current page number is displayed at the far left; if the printed notebook consisted of more than one page, you would move among pages by clicking on the right and left arrows or by pressing [Pg Dn] and [Pg Up]. To the right of the arrows is the current **zoom level.** On the display area, the mouse pointer turns into a magnifying glass. Click with the left mouse button or press the plus symbol ([+]) to zoom in to the notebook and show more detail. Click with the right mouse button or press the minus symbol ([-]) to zoom out and show less detail.

2. Position the mouse on the displayed notebook and click until the zoom level reads "1600%".

3. Right-click until the zoom level reads "100%".

The Preview screen shows you that the appearance of the printed notebook has improved. The columns line up properly and the information in the header and footer is printed only once, not four times. But there is still room for improvement. Wouldn't it be better to display the information on total expenses further up the page, rather than right at the bottom? And to print the header and footer in bold letters, to set them off from the rest of the page?

You can make both changes from the Spreadsheet Page Setup dialog box. Rather than going back to the notebook to select Page Setup from the File menu, however, you can select it by clicking on the Page Setup button on the Preview SpeedBar (refer to Figure 9-2).

Adjusting Margins

1. Click on the Page Setup button.

In order to move the footer further up the page, you will need to increase the bottom margin.

NOTE: Quattro Pro for Windows measures the bottom, top, and side margins from the edge of the paper. The header measurements are calculated from the top margin; the footer measurements are calculated from the bottom margin.

2. Click on the Bottom edit field (refer to Figure 9-1) and edit it to read "4.50 in".

Changing Header Font Attributes

1. To display the header and footer in bold letters, click on the Header Font button. The Select Font dialog box appears (see Figure 9-3).

2. Click on Bold, under Options, then click on OK. You are returned to the Spreadsheet Page Setup dialog box.

3. Click on OK to return to the preview screen.

Printing from the Preview Screen

That looks better. You can print from the Preview screen by clicking on the Print button on the SpeedBar (refer to Figure 9-2).

Figure 9-3
Changing the header font

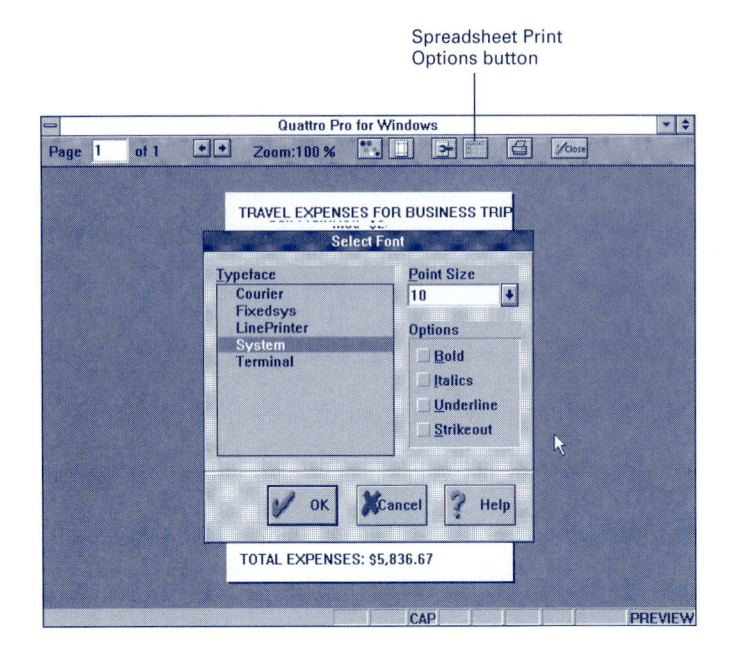

1. Click on the Print button on the SpeedBar. A message appears informing you that the notebook is being printed. If you wish to stop printing for some reason, click on the Cancel button.

After the notebook is printed, you are returned to the Preview screen. If you want to make additional changes, do so now. When finished, click on the Close button on the SpeedBar (refer to Figure 9-3) to return to the notebook.

2. Click on the Close button. You are returned to the Spreadsheet Print dialog box.

3. Click on Close to return to the notebook.

4. Turn off Group mode by clicking on the Group button.

SAVING PRINT SETTINGS

One way to save print settings is to save the notebook. The settings are saved automatically, so that next time you want to print it, you do not need to specify them again. But suppose you want to print the notebook in a different form next time? How can you save several different print settings for the same notebook? The answer is that you can use File | Named Settings and choose a name for each setting you want to save. You can then reset the print settings to their default values so you can create a new print setting next time.

Follow these steps to give the current print settings a name:

1. Select File | Named Settings. The Named Print Settings dialog box will appear (see Figure 9-4).

Figure 9-4
Saving print settings

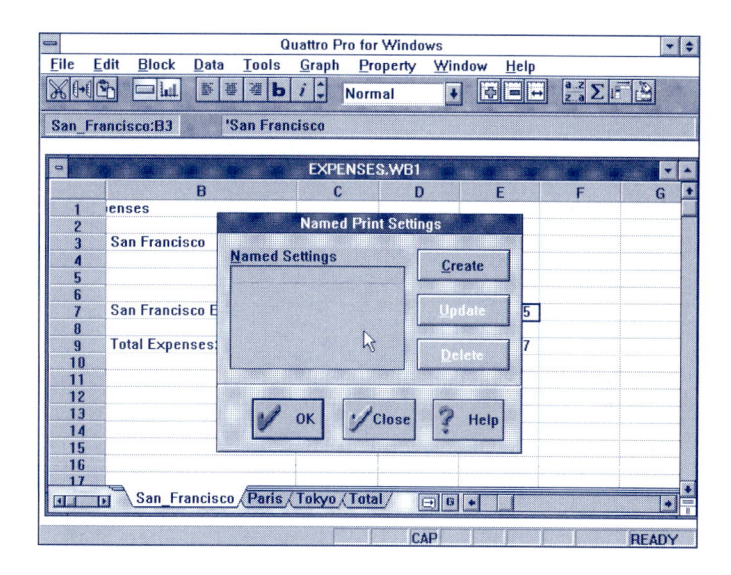

2. Click on Create. Type **One page** and press Enter. You are returned to the Named Print Settings dialog box.

3. Click on OK. The current settings are saved under the name "One page".

To print using the named settings, select File | Named Settings and select the setting you want to use, then select File | Print and print the notebook.

SELECTING A MULTIPLE-PAGE PRINT BLOCK

In this section, you will learn other printing techniques. Since you are finished with EXPENSES.WB1, save it, then retrieve VACATION.WB1.

1. Select File | Save.

2. Select File | Retrieve and choose VACATION.WB1.

3. Press Home to move to A1, if you are not there already.

You did not create this notebook with grouped pages, but you can still print both pages at the same time. The technique is to hold down Shift with one hand while specifying a block that is spread over more than one page.

Follow these steps to select the block to print:

1. Move to A3 in Prices by clicking on it.
2. While holding down [Shift]:
   a. Click on C22 to select cells A3..C22. Release the mouse button.
   b. Click on the Monthly_Payment tab to make that page the active page. A dark line will appear below the Prices and Monthly_Payments tabs, indicating that both have been selected. Cells A3..C22 will be highlighted.
   c. Extend the highlight through D22 by clicking on D22.
3. Release [Shift].

Printing Notebook Pages Separately

Because of the way the notebook is set up, both pages will print on one page. To tell Quattro Pro for Windows to keep the pages separate, use Page Advance from the Print Options dialog box. You can select Options from the File Print dialog box, but you can also select it by clicking on the Options SpeedBar button from the Preview screen.

1. Select File | Print, then click on the Preview button.
2. Click on the Spreadsheet Print Options button on the SpeedBar (refer to Figure 9-3). The Spreadsheet Print Options dialog box is displayed (see Figure 9-5).

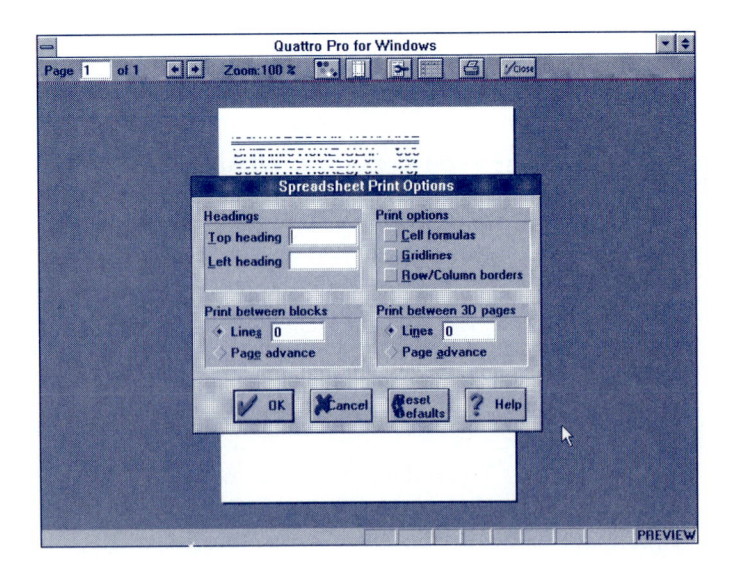

Figure 9-5
Changing print options

3. Click on Page Advance.

4. Click on OK to return to the Preview screen.

Alignment, Dates, and Page Numbers in Headers and Footers

The next step is to specify the header and footer. You want to enter VACATION PARADISE as the header and today's date and the page number as the footer. In addition, you would like to center the header, left-align the date, and right-align the page number.

To enter today's date and the page number, as well as to change alignment, you must use special symbols. In a header or footer,

When you type:	Quattro Pro for Windows will:
#	print the page number
@	print the date
no vertical bar	left-align the text you enter
¦	center the text you enter
¦ ¦	right-align the text you enter

To enter the header:

1. Click on the Page Setup button on the SpeedBar.

2. Click on the Header edit field and type ¦ **VACATION PARADISE**. The vertical bar tells Quattro Pro for Windows that the text should be centered.

3. Click on the Footer edit field (or press [Tab]) and type @¦ ¦**page #**. The "at" symbol (@) tells Quattro Pro for Windows to print the date, left-aligned; the two vertical lines followed by "page #" tell Quattro Pro for Windows to print the word "page" followed by the page number, right-aligned.

4. Click on OK to return to the Preview screen. As you can see, the header and footer have been added. The footer on page 1 reads "page 1".

   a. Click on the right arrow on the SpeedBar to see that the footer on page 2 reads "page 2".

   b. Click on the left arrow on the SpeedBar to return to page 1.

If you want to make additional changes, do so now.

5. Print the notebook by clicking on the Print button.

6. Click on Close to return to the Spreadsheet Print dialog box; click on Close again to return to the notebook.

Having printed the VACATION.WB1 notebook, you are ready to move on to the next section.

1. Select File ¦ Save.

2. Select File ¦ Retrieve and choose BOOK.WB1.

CREATING HEADINGS FROM ROW AND COLUMN LABELS

In this example, you will first print the notebook using column titles as headings in addition to an overall header ("Bookstore Spreadsheet and Graphs") and a footer showing the date. Then you will print the graphs with the same header by selecting them from the Graphs page.

To set up the column titles as headings for the printed notebook data, use the Top Heading edit field on the Print Options dialog box to point to the block you wish to use as the heading.

1. Select File ¦ Print and click on the Options button.

Notice that there are two edit fields in the upper left of the dialog box, one for a **Top heading** and one for a **Left heading.** A top heading consists of one or more rows and will print at the top of each page of the notebook report. It is useful when you have too many rows to print on one page and want to make sure that each column is properly identified. For example, if you had 150 books in BOOK.WB1, Quattro Pro for Windows would not be able to fit them all on one page. Using A3..E3 (the block with column titles) as a top heading would ensure that column titles appear above the columns on each page of the report. A left heading consists of one or more columns and will print at the left side of each page. It is useful when you have many columns to print and want to make sure each row is properly identified. For example, if in addition to TITLE, PRICE, UNIT SALES, and TOTAL SALES for each book you also had NAME, ADDRESS, and TELEPHONE NUMBER for each author, Quattro Pro for Windows would not be able to print all the columns on one page. The information on TITLE, PRICE, UNIT SALES, TOTAL SALES, and NAME would be printed on one page, and ADDRESS and TELEPHONE NUMBER would be printed on the next. You would have to paste the two pages together to figure out which author went with each book. If you specified the columns with the book number and title as a left heading, though, that information would be printed on all pages of the report.

For this example, you will specify a top heading.

2. Double-click on the Top heading edit field to enter Point mode and select A3..E3. Then click on the Maximize button on the Spreadsheet Print Options title bar. The top heading block is now defined.

3. Click on OK to return to the Spreadsheet Print dialog box.

Next specify the block to be printed. In this case, since you have specified A3 through E3 as the top heading block, do not include it for the printing block, or the title and column labels will be printed twice. Instead specify A4 through E13.

4. Double-click on the Print block edit field to enter Point mode and select A4..E13. Then click on the Maximize button on the Spreadsheet Print title bar.

5. To specify the header and footer, click on Close to leave the Spreadsheet Print dialog box and select File | Page Setup.

6. Click on Header and type **Bookstore Spreadsheet and Graphs**

7. For the footer, click on Footer and type @

8. Click on OK.

9. Select File | Print and click on Print. The notebook page will be printed.

PRINTING A GRAPH FROM THE GRAPHS PAGE

You already know how to print graphs from a spreadsheet page. Printing graphs from the Graphs page is very similar: Simply select the graph and select File | Print. The advantage of printing from the Graphs page is that you can select several graphs at once and print them with one command. You can also specify headers and footers.

To illustrate these features, you will print the Book Prices, Book Sales, and Total Sales graphs from the Graphs page. You will give each the same header and footer you gave the notebook data.

1. Click on the SpeedTab button to move to the Graphs page. Icons of the three graphs you have created should be on the page.

2. To select all three graphs (Book Prices, Book Sales, and Total Sales), hold down [Shift] with one hand while clicking on each in turn. All three should be highlighted.

3. Release [Shift].

Adding Headers and Footers to Graphs

The procedure for adding a header or footer to a graph or a set of graphs is similar to what you have already learned.

1. Select File | Page Setup. The Graph Page Setup dialog box is displayed.

2. Click on Header and type **Bookstore Spreadsheet and Graphs**

3. Click on Footer and type @

4. Click on OK.

To print the graphs:

1. Select File | Print. To preview the graphs, click on Preview and click on the arrows or press [Pg Up] and [Pg Dn] to examine each page.

2. When done, click on the Print button on the SpeedBar (refer to Figure 9-2), then on the Close button to return to the Spreadsheet Print dialog box.

3. Click on Close to return to the Graphs page.

This concludes the lesson and the book. I hope you have enjoyed your first look at Quattro Pro for Windows. By now you should be familiar with many of its most important features. You should be able to use it in your own applications and begin to find out for yourself how Quattro Pro for Windows can make your work easier.

■ SUMMARY OF COMMANDS

Topic or Feature	Command or Reference	Menu	Page
Select a Block Across Grouped Pages	Click on the Group button, then select the block		136
Add Headers and Footers	Page Setup button from the Preview screen	File	Page Setup	136, 139
Center a Block on a Page	Page Setup button from the Preview screen	File	Page Setup	137, 138
Preview	Preview button from the File	Print dialog box	File	Print Preview	138
Zoom In to Preview	Left-click or type [+]		138
Zoom Out to Preview	Right-click or type [−]		138
Preview the Next Page	Click on the SpeedBar arrow or press [Pg Dn]		138
Preview the Previous Page	Click on the SpeedBar arrow or press [Pg Up]		138

Lesson 9 / Printing Notebooks and Graphs   **147**

Topic or Feature	Command or Reference	Menu	Page
Margins	Page Setup button from the Preview screen	File ¦ Page Setup	139
Font Attributes in Headers and Footers	Page Setup button from the Preview screen, then the Header Font button	File ¦ Page Setup, then the Header Font button	139
Print the Selected Notebook Pages	Print button from the Preview screen	File ¦ Print	139
Save Print Settings		File ¦ Named Settings	140
Select a Block Across Multiple Pages	Hold down [Shift] while selecting the block on each page in succession		141
Print Notebook Pages Separately	Options button from the File Print dialog box or the Preview screen		142
Center Headers and Footers	Page Setup button from the Preview screen, then ¦		143
Right-align Headers and Footers	Page Setup button from the Preview screen, then ¦ ¦		143
Print Page Numbers in Headers and Footers	Page Setup button from the Preview screen, then #		143
Print Dates in Headers and Footers	Page Setup button from the Preview screen, then @		143
Create Headings from Row and Column Labels	Options button from the File Print dialog box or the Preview screen		144
Select Multiple Graphs from the Graphs Page	Hold down [Shift] while clicking on each graph in turn		145
Print Graphs from the Graphs Page	Print button from the Preview screen	File ¦ Print from the Graphs page	145
Add Headers and Footers to Graphs	Page Setup button from the Preview screen	File ¦ Page Setup from the Graphs page	145

148 First Look at Quattro Pro for Windows

■ REVIEW QUESTIONS

1. Your notebook extends from A:A1 through C:C15, and pages A through C are defined as group Alpha. What steps would you follow to print it on a single page?

2. Your notebook extends from B:A1 through D:C15, and pages B through D are defined as group Bet. What steps would you follow to print each page on a separate page?

3. Your notebook consists of two pages, A:A1..G6 and B:B1..D9. They are not defined as a group. What steps would you follow to print them both on one page?

4. What features discussed in this lesson are found on the Spreadsheet Page Setup dialog box?

5. What features discussed in this lesson are found on the Spreadsheet Print Options dialog box?

6. What features discussed in this lesson are found on the Graph Page Setup dialog box?

7. Explain the difference between the Header edit field and the Headings edit fields.

8. Identify the following SpeedBar buttons from the Preview screen:

■ HANDS-ON EXERCISES

Print the notebooks you have developed in the Hands-on Exercises from the previous lessons. Use Preview to make sure the notebooks are set up properly before printing them.

Exercise 9-1

1. Print NANNY.WB1 on a single page. Add a descriptive header and a footer with the date and page number. Center all text.

2. Print the notebook you created in Lesson Five (CARS1.WB1, CARS2.WB1, or CARS3.WB1), placing each page and graph on a separate sheet of paper. Add the same descriptive header and a footer with the date and page number. Make both header and footer boldface.

3. Print PRINTER.WB1. Use the column labels as the top headings and the printer manufacturers as the left headings. Add a footer with the page number to the notebook pages and to the graphs.

Exercise 9-2

Use the spreadsheet skills you have learned to print the notebook you created in Lessons Three and Four (WOOL1.WB1, WOOL2.WB1, or WOOL3.WB1) as clearly as possible. Include a descriptive header and a footer with the date and page number.

NOTE: If your notebook pages have too many columns to fit on a single page, Quattro Pro for Windows will divide them into two pages. Two ways to deal with this are to edit the notebook or to use left headings. Can you think of other ways?

Exercise 9-3

This exercise builds on Lesson Eight, Exercise 8-2. Your boss has asked you to hand in a report on the supplies you have ordered. Design and print the notebook to display the information—and your spreadsheet skills—to best advantage.

Answers to Review Questions

LESSON 1

1. The standard features of a spreadsheet are the ability to carry out calculations and analyze different scenarios for decision making.
2. Quattro Pro for Windows' new features include use of the mouse to move and edit data, shortcuts for selecting frequently used commands, easy formatting of spreadsheet contents, enhanced graphs and charts, a quick and intuitive way to link many spreadsheets together, and presentation-quality spreadsheet printing.
3. It has the usual keys for typing, but instead of appearing on paper, the words appear on the computer monitor. It also has special keys that are used in computer programs.
4. As you move a mouse on a desktop or other flat surface, the mouse pointer on the monitor moves.
5. When the mouse pointer is correctly positioned, you can click, right-click, double-click, or drag to work with programs.
6. Windows gets its name from the window metaphor: Each program on your disk appears in a box called a "window," which you can open, close, or resize.
7. Computers can be set up in different ways, which can affect how you start Windows. Windows may start automatically when you turn on the computer. Or you may be able to select it from a menu.
8. When you start Windows, you see the Windows desktop.
9. An icon is a small symbol that represents program features. In Windows, icons are used to represent program groups or programs.
10. Drag the mouse to move an icon.
11. Double-click to open a program group.
12. Double-click to start a program.
13. To select a menu item, click on it. To close a menu, click on the background to it or press [Esc]
14. Use the Maximize (▲), Minimize (▼), or Restore (◆) buttons on the title bar; or position the mouse so that the pointer turns into a double-headed arrow, then drag the sides of the window with the mouse until the window is the desired size.
15. It is found on the menu bar in the File Manager.

LESSON 2

1. The four parts are the notebook, SpeedBar, menu bar, and title bar.
2. Quattro Pro for Windows gives the notebook the name NOTEBK1.WB1.
3. Pages are designated by letters in alphabetical order.
4. Columns are designated by letters in alphabetical order.
5. Rows are designated by numbers in ascending order.
6. A cell is the intersection of a row and a column; it gets its cell address from the letter of its page, the letter of its column, and the number of its row.
7. Scroll through pages, scroll through rows, scroll through columns, make a page the active page, and display cell contents in boldface.
8. Move one screen down (through rows), move one screen up (through rows), move one screen to the right (through columns), move one screen to the left (through columns), move to A1.
9. Enter Edit mode by pressing [F2]; it allows you to edit existing cell contents.
10. A label consists of alphanumeric characters (text); a value is a number or an expression that can represent a number.
11. To delete the contents of a cell, position the cell selector on it, then press [Del]
12. The SpeedBar is the row of buttons above the notebook, each of which carries out a frequently used command.
13. To choose a command from the menu bar, click on the menu heading, then on the command; from the keyboard, type [/], then press the underlined or highlighted letter.
14. To close up a menu, click on the background to the menu or click outside the menu box; or press [Esc]
15. Select File ¦ Save to save a spreadsheet notebook.
16. Select File ¦ Close to close a spreadsheet notebook.
17. Select File ¦ Exit to exit Quattro Pro for Windows.

LESSON 3

1. Select the cells by dragging the mouse. Then hold down Ctrl while dragging the block outline to the desired location. Release the left mouse button, then release Ctrl.
2. To enter the formula, type +, click on B1, type +, click on C3, then press Enter.
3. A relative cell address in a formula locates a cell by its position with respect to the formula; an absolute cell address in a formula locates a cell at a specific cell address, regardless of its position with respect to the formula.
4. The F4 key inserts dollar signs into an absolute cell address.
5. Select a block consisting of the column of numbers and the blank cell immediately below it or to the right, then click on the SpeedSum button on the SpeedBar.
6. The function is @SUM() and B1..B6 is the cell block to be operated on. The function will add up all the values in cells B1 through B6 inclusive and put the sum in the cell in which the function is located.
7. Press Alt-F3 to call up the Function menu.
8. Object Inspector menus are context-sensitive menus displayed in dialog boxes or lists that allow you to change the properties of a cell, block, graph feature, or page. You display the menus by right-clicking on the cell, block, graph feature, or page to be modified.
9. Click on the cell to select it, right-click to display Object Inspector menus, click on Currency from Numeric Format, specify the number of decimal places, and click on OK.
10. Select the column by clicking on the column letter button, then click on the Fit button on the SpeedBar.
11. Select the block, then press Del.

LESSON 4

1. The buttons are Cut, Copy, Paste, Bold, Italic, Insert, Delete, Fit, and SpeedSum.
2. Select File | Open to open a notebook. You *open* an existing notebook; you *create* a new notebook by entering data into a blank notebook.
3. Click on the row number to select the row; click on the column letter to select the column.
4. They appear below the selected row.
5. They appear to the right of the selected column.
6. Yes. The new formula will be +B8*K20.
7. No, the formula will remain the same.
8. No, the formula will remain the same.
9. Select E5..G5, right-click to display the Object Inspector menu, click on Line Drawing, click on the double line under Line Types, click on the bottom line under Line Segments, and click on OK.
10. Select File | Print, make sure the Print block edit field is set correctly, and click on the Print button.
11. It must be set for A:A1..C15.

LESSON 5

1. Click on any cell in the column, right-click to display the Object Inspector menu, click on Column Width, type the desired width, and click on OK.
2. Press Shift-F7 and use the arrow keys and Pg Up and Pg Dn to extend the block.
3. Click on the cell to select it and right-click to display the Object Inspector menu. The default choice is Numeric Format; click on Comma or Percent to choose those formats, enter the desired number of decimal places, and click on OK.
4. Click on the cell to select it, right-click to display the Object Inspector menu, click on Alignment, click on Right or Center, and click on OK.
5. The @COUNT() function is used to calculate the number of nonblank cells in a block; @MAX() is used to calculate the highest value in a block; @MIN() is used to calculate the lowest value in a block; @PMT() is used to calculate loan payments, given the principal, the interest rate, and the number of payment periods.
6. A conditional statement is one where the result depends on whether a given condition is true or not. Use it in a spreadsheet to set up what-if scenarios.
7. Use @IF. Include the condition, what to do if the condition is met, and what to do if the condition is not met.
8. Enter +A1.
9. Enter the following function:
   @IF(B6=your weekly salary/3,"Eureka!","Oops!")

LESSON 6

1. Information is organized into fields and records.
2. Each field must be placed in a separate column; each record must be placed on a separate row.
3. When you want to give each record an identification number.
4. The three pieces of information are the Start value, the Step value, and the Stop value.
5. The purpose is to let Quattro Pro for Windows know that the column labels are field names.
6. A key field is the field by which the database is sorted. Use it when sorting a database.
7. A criteria table is a block of cells that specifies search criteria.
8. Locate is used to locate all database records that fit the given criteria; Extract is used to extract information from all records that fit the given criteria and copy it to a new section of the notebook.
9. An output block is a section of the notebook where database information that fits certain criteria is placed.
10. Select Data ¦ Query, double-click on the edit field, select the block from the notebook, then click on the Maximize button on the dialog box title bar to return to the dialog box.

LESSON 7

1. Select the block containing the data to be graphed, click on the Graph tool on the SpeedBar, then select the section of the notebook page to insert the graph.
2. You can quickly create a graph of your data and quickly print it by selecting File ¦ Print. You can select, move, copy, paste, or delete it as you would a cell block.
3. The Graph menu allows you to carefully design and edit a graph that displays complex data to best advantage.
4. Select Graph ¦ Type and click on the desired graph type.
5. A series is a block of data (values or labels) used in creating a graph.
6. Three types are pie, rotated bar, and line. Use pie charts to display data as percentages of a whole; use rotated bar graphs to compare a series of items; use a line graph to show the relationship among series.
7. You can specify six Y-series.
8. You can specify one X-series.
9. Be careful to place the mouse pointer precisely on the part of the graph you want to modify.
10. The graph is not saved.

LESSON 8

1. Select the block, click on the Cut button on the SpeedBar, move to the new page, and click on the Paste button.
2. Select the block, click on the Copy button on the SpeedBar, move to the new page, and click on the Paste button.
3. The function will be @COUNT(A:B10..A:B25).
4. The function will be @COUNT(B:A1..B:A16).
5. The function will be @COUNT($A:$B$10..$A:$B$25).
6. Position the mouse pointer on the upper part of the Screen Splitter to divide the screen horizontally and on the lower part to divide the screen vertically. Press the left mouse button and move the dotted line to the place you want to split the screen, then release the left mouse button.
7. Use File ¦ Retrieve when you want to close one file and open another in one step.
8. To move a block, select the block, then drag it to the new location. To copy a block, select the block, then hold down [Ctrl] while dragging it to a new location.
9. First, click on the first page of the group, then hold down [Shift] and click on the last page of the group. Release [Shift]. Then select Tools ¦ Define Group.
10. Hold down [Ctrl] while using the mouse to select each part of the block in turn, then release [Ctrl].
11. Click on the Group button to enter Group mode.
12. While in Group mode, any operation you carry out on one page will be carried out on all pages in the group.

LESSON 9

1. Click on the Group button to enter Group mode, select A1..C15 on page A, select File ¦ Print, and click on the Print button.
2. Click on the Group button to enter Group mode, select A1..C15 on page B, select File ¦ Print, click on the Options button, click on Page Advance, click on OK, and click on the Print button.
3. Click on A. While holding down [Shift], select A1..G6, click on B, select B1..D9, then release [Shift]. Select File ¦ Print and click on the Print button.
4. The features are header, footer, margins, center blocks, and header font.
5. The features are headings and page advance.
6. The features are header and footer.
7. The Header edit field on the Spreadsheet Page Setup dialog box allows you to type in text for a new header. The Headings edit fields on the Spreadsheet Print Options dialog box allow you to use existing row and column labels as headings.
8. Page Setup button, Print Options button, Print button, and Close button.

Quattro Pro for Windows Reference and Command Summary

This section is a quick reference for Quattro Pro for Windows commands and features. It is not a complete list of Quattro Pro for Windows commands, but it does contain frequently used commands not discussed in the book.

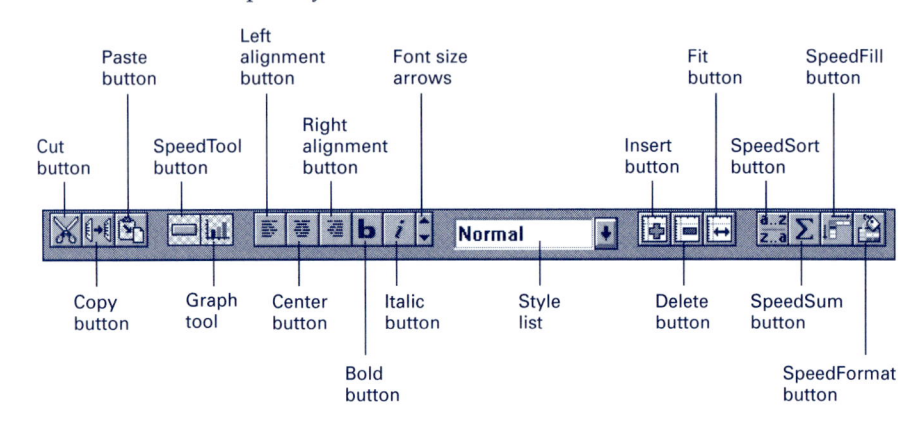

Notebook SpeedBar

Callouts (top): Paste button, Left alignment button, Font size arrows, Fit button, SpeedFill button, Cut button, SpeedTool button, Right alignment button, Insert button, SpeedSort button

Callouts (bottom): Copy button, Graph tool, Center button, Italic button, Style list, Delete button, SpeedSum button, Bold button, SpeedFormat button

Data Entry SpeedBar

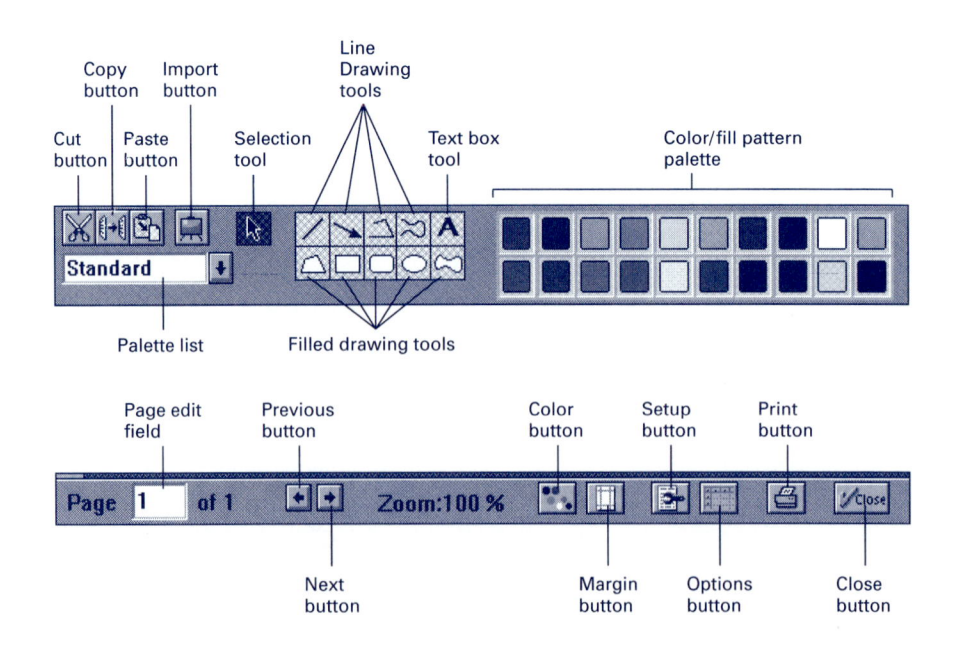

Callouts: Functions button, Macros button

Graph SpeedBar

Callouts (top): Copy button, Import button, Line Drawing tools, Cut button, Paste button, Selection tool, Text box tool, Color/fill pattern palette

Callouts (bottom): Palette list, Filled drawing tools

Print Preview SpeedBar

Callouts (top): Page edit field, Previous button, Color button, Setup button, Print button

Callouts (bottom): Next button, Margin button, Options button, Close button

154

Quattro Pro for Windows Reference and Command Summary 155

Topic or Feature	Command	Menu	Page

Calculating Tools

+	Plus		28
-	Minus		28
*	Multiplied by		28
/	Divided by		28
<	Less than		28
>	Greater than		28
=	Equal to		28
<>	Not equal to		28
( )	Group expressions		28
@AVG(cell block)	Calculates the average of the values in the cell block; [Alt]-[F3], select AVG		
@COUNT(cell block)	Counts the number of nonblank cells in the block; [Alt]-[F3], select COUNT		76
@IF(condition, action if condition is true, action if condition is false)	Evaluates a conditional statement and carries out an action; [Alt]-[F3], select IF		81
@MAX(cell block)	Calculates the maximum value in a block; [Alt]-[F3], select MAX		76
@MIN(cell block)	Calculates the minimum value in a block; [Alt]-[F3], select MIN		76
@PMT(principal, rate, number of periods)	Calculates the payments per period; [Alt]-[F3], select PMT		77
@SUM(cell block)	Adds the values in a block; [Alt]-[F3], select SUM		45
Solve for the Conditions Necessary to Produce the Desired Result of a Formula		Tools ¦ Solve For	

Command Menu

Choose a Menu Command	Click on the menu bar heading, then on the item		30
Close a Menu	Click on the background, or press [Esc]		9, 31
Pull Down a Menu	Click on the heading, or press [/], then the highlighted letter in the heading		30

Cursor Movement Keys

[→]	Moves right one cell		25
[←]	Moves left one cell		25
[↑]	Moves up one cell		25
[↓]	Moves down one cell		25
[Pg Up]	Moves up one screen		25
[Pg Dn]	Moves down one screen		25
[Ctrl]-[←]	Moves one screen to the left		25
[Ctrl]-[→]	Moves one screen to the right		25
[Home]	Moves the cursor to A1 of the active page		25
[F5]	GoTo key; prompts for a cell address to move to	Edit ¦ Goto	
Make a New Page the Active Page	Click on the page tab		23

Topic or Feature	Command	Menu	Page
Move Among Columns	Column scroll bar		25
Move Among Pages	Page scroll bar		23
Move Among Rows	Row scroll bar		25
Move to Graphs Page	SpeedTab button		

Database Commands

Topic or Feature	Command	Menu	Page
Assign Names to Database Fields	Field Names button	Data ǀ Query	91
Criteria Table	Criteria Table edit field	Data ǀ Query	94
Extract Records That Meet Specified Criteria	Extract button	Data ǀ Query	95
Locate Records That Meet Specified Criteria	Locate button	Data ǀ Query	94
Output Block	Output Block edit field	Data ǀ Query	95
Reset Data Query	Reset button	Data ǀ Query	96
Sort a Database		Data ǀ Sort	92
Sort Keys	1st through 5th edit fields	Data ǀ Sort	92

Entering and Editing Data

Topic or Feature	Command	Menu	Page
Absolute Cell Addresses	F4		44
Alignment of Labels	Right-click on the cell or block to be modified, then click on Alignment; Alignment buttons on the SpeedBar	Object Inspector menus	73
Boldface	Bold button on the SpeedBar		29
Column Width	Right-click on the cell or block to be modified, then click on Column Width; Fit button on the SpeedBar	Object Inspector menus	71
Comma (Financial) Format	Right-click on the cell or block to be modified, then click on Numeric Format, Comma	Object Inspector menus	73
Copy a Cell Block	Copy button on the SpeedBar; hold down Ctrl while dragging the block with the mouse	Edit ǀ Copy; Block ǀ Copy	40, 60
Copy a Cell or Block	Copy and Paste buttons on the SpeedBar	Edit ǀ Copy; Block ǀ Copy	40, 60
Copy a Cell or Block Between Pages	Copy button on the SpeedBar	Edit ǀ Copy; Block ǀ Copy	126
Currency Format	Right-click on the cell or block to be modified, then click on Numeric Format, Currency	Object Inspector menus	48
Cut a Cell or Block	Cut button on the SpeedBar	Edit ǀ Cut	
Delete a Block	Select a block, then click on the Delete button on the SpeedBar	Block ǀ Delete; Edit ǀ Clear Contents	41
Delete a Column	Select a column, then click on the Delete button on the SpeedBar	Block ǀ Delete ǀ Columns	59
Delete a Page	Click on the page tab, then click on the Delete button on the SpeedBar	Block ǀ Delete ǀ Pages	
Delete a Row	Select a row, then click on the Delete button on the SpeedBar	Block ǀ Delete ǀ Rows	57
Delete Cell Contents	Del	Edit ǀ Clear Contents	28
Delete Cell Contents and Format		Edit ǀ Clear	

Quattro Pro for Windows Reference and Command Summary   157

Topic or Feature	Command	Menu	Page
Draw Lines and Boxes	Right-click on the cell or block to be modified, then click on Line Drawing	Object Inspector menus	63
Edit Cell Contents	[F2]		25
Enter Blocks in Edit Fields with Point Mode	Double-click on the edit field		97
Function Menu	[Alt]-[F3] or the @ button on the SpeedBar		46
Insert a Block	Select a block, then click on the Insert button on the SpeedBar	Block ¦ Insert	
Insert a Column	Select a column, then click on the Insert button on the SpeedBar	Block ¦ Insert ¦ Columns	58
Insert a Page	Click on the page tab, then click on the Insert button on the SpeedBar	Block ¦ Insert ¦ Pages	
Insert a Row	Select a row, then click on the Insert button on the SpeedBar	Block ¦ Insert ¦ Rows	57
Italics	Italic button on the SpeedBar		29
Move a Block	Drag with the mouse	Block ¦ Move	126
Move a Cell or Block	Cut and Paste buttons on the SpeedBar	Block ¦ Move	63, 119
Move a Floating Graph	Drag with the mouse		
Move a Graph Icon	Drag with the mouse		
Move Between Pages	Click on the page tab		
Move Between Windows	Click on any cell in a window to make it the active window		122
Move Pages	Drag the page tab with the mouse to the desired position	Block ¦ Move Pages	
Numeric Format	Right-click on the cell or block to be modified, then click on Numeric Format	Object Inspector menus, from the cell or block	74, 77
Page Names	Right-click on the page tab	Object Inspector menus, from the page tab	120
Paste a Cell or Block	Paste button on the SpeedBar	Edit ¦ Paste	
Percent Format	Right-click on the cell or block to be modified, then click on Numeric Format, Percent	Object Inspector menus	77
Select a Block	Drag the mouse; press [Shift]-[F7]		39, 72
Select a Block Across Grouped Pages	Click on the Group button, then select the block		136
Select a Block Across Multiple Pages	Hold down [Shift] while selecting the block on each page in succession		141
Select a Cell	Click on it		
Select a Column	Click on the column letter button		58
Select a Floating Graph	Click on it		
Select a Graph Icon	Click on it		
Select a Page	Click on the Select All box at the intersection of row and column borders		
Select a Row	Click on the row number button		57
Select Multiple Graphs from the Graphs Page	Hold down [Shift] while clicking on each graph in turn		145
Select Noncontiguous Blocks	Hold down [Ctrl] while selecting each block in turn		128
Sequential values		Block ¦ Fill	89

158   First Look at Quattro Pro for Windows

Topic or Feature	Command	Menu	Page
Sort a Block	SpeedSort button on the SpeedBar		74
Split the Screen into Two Windows	Drag the Screen Splitter		122
Sum a Column or Row of Values	SpeedSum button on the SpeedBar	@SUM() function from the Function menu; [Alt]-[F3]	45
Undo the Most Recent Action		Edit ¦ Undo	
Files			
Close All Open Notebooks		File ¦ Close All	
Close a Notebook		File ¦ Close	33
Close the Active Notebook and Open an Existing Notebook		File ¦ Retrieve	124
Create a New Notebook		File ¦ New	38
Exit Quattro Pro for Windows	[Alt]-[F4]	File ¦ Exit	33
Open an Existing Notebook	Click on a file from the list, then click on OK	File ¦ Open	55
Save All Open Notebooks		File ¦ Save All	
Save a Notebook		File ¦ Save	32
Save a Notebook with a New Name		File ¦ Save As	
Graphs			
Copy a Graph		Graph ¦ Copy	
Create a Floating Graph	Select the data, then click on the Graph tool on the SpeedBar		103
Create a New Graph		Graph ¦ New	106
Delete a Floating Graph	Click on it, then press [Del]		104
Delete a Graph		Graph ¦ Delete	
Edit a Floating Graph	Right-click on the graph	Object Inspector menus	
Edit an Existing Graph		Graph ¦ Edit	109
Edit Graph Series		Graph ¦ Series	108
Graph and Series Titles		Graph ¦ Titles	109
Modify Graph Titles		Graph ¦ Titles	109
Modify Graph Type		Graph ¦ Type	103
Move a Floating Graph	Drag it to the desired position		104
Name an Existing Graph	Right-click on the graph icon on the Graphs page	Object Inspector menus, from the graph icon on the Graphs page	110
Print a Floating Graph		File ¦ Print	104
Print a Graph		File ¦ Print	114
Restore a Graph to an Icon on the Graphs Page	Click on the Close button or the Minimize button (▼)	Control menu/Close	110
Save a Graph	Save the notebook	File ¦ Save	114
Select a Floating Graph	Click on it		104

Quattro Pro for Windows Reference and Command Summary   **159**

Topic or Feature	Command	Menu	Page
Series Labels	Right-click on graph series, then enter the block for labels	Object Inspector menus, from graph series	111
Specify Series for a New Graph		Graph ǀ New	106
Text Font for Series Labels	Right-click on the series labels, then click on Text Font	Object Inspector menus, from series labels	
View a Graph		Graph ǀ View	
View a Graph from the Graphs Page	Double-click on the graph icon		110

Grouped Pages

Topic or Feature	Command	Menu	Page
Add Cell Contents Across Grouped Pages	Click on the Group button, then use SpeedSum from the SpeedBar		130
Define a Group of Pages	Click on the first page of a group, hold down [Shift], then click on the last page of the group	Tools ǀ Define Group	127
Group Mode	Click on the Group button		128
Paste Cell Contents to All Pages in a Group	Click on the Group button, then use the Paste button from the SpeedBar		129
Select a Block Across Grouped Pages	Click on the Group button, then select the block		136

Help

Topic or Feature	Command	Menu	Page
Help with Any Feature	Select the feature or command, then press [F1]		

Mouse Actions

Topic or Feature	Command	Menu	Page
Copy a Block	Hold down [Ctrl] while dragging the block to the new location	Block ǀ Copy	40
Modify the Features of an Object (cell, block, page, graph) with Object Inspector Menus	Right-click on the object to be modified	Object Inspector menus	47
Move a Selected Object (cell, block, page, graph)	Drag the selected object to the new location		
Move Between Pages	Click on the page tab		119
Move Between Windows	Click on any cell in a window to make it the active window		122
Resize Windows	Click on the Maximize, Minimize, or Restore buttons, or drag the sides of the window to the desired size		9, 10
Select a Block	Move to the first cell in the block, then drag the mouse to the last cell in the block		72
Select a Block Across Grouped Pages	Click on the Group button, then select the block		
Select a Block Across Multiple Pages	Hold down [Shift] while selecting the block on each page in succession		141
Select an Object (cell, block, graph)	Click on the object		
Select Multiple Graphs from the Graphs Page	Hold down [Shift] while clicking on each graph in turn		145
Select Noncontiguous blocks	Hold down [Ctrl] while selecting each block in turn		128

Topic or Feature	Command	Menu	Page
Start a Program in Windows	Double-click on the program icon		12
Printing			
Center a Block on the Page	Page Setup button from the Preview screen	File | Page Setup	137, 138
Center Headers and Footers	Page Setup button from the Preview screen, then |	File | Page Setup	143
Dates in Headers and Footers	Page Setup button from the Preview screen, then @	File | Page Setup	143
Font Attributes in Headers and Footers	Page Setup button from the Preview screen, then the Header Font button	File | Page Setup, then the Header Font button	139
Footers	Page Setup button from the Preview screen	File | Page Setup	136, 139
Footers with Graphs	Page Setup button from the Preview screen	File | Page Setup from the Graphs page	145
Headers	Page Setup button from the Preview screen	File | Page Setup	136, 139
Headers with Graphs	Page Setup button from the Preview screen	File | Page Setup from the Graphs page	145
Headings from Row and Column Labels	Options button from the File Print dialog box or the Preview screen	File | Print	144
Margins	Page Setup button from the Preview screen	File | Page Setup	139
Page Numbers in Headers and Footers	Page Setup button from the Preview screen, then #	File | Page Setup	143
Preview	Preview button from the File Print dialog box	File | Print Preview	138
Preview the Next Page	Click on the SpeedBar arrow or press [Pg Dn]		138
Preview the Previous Page	Click on the SpeedBar arrow or press [Pg Up]		138
Print	Print button from the Preview screen	File | Print	138
Print Graphs from the Graphs Page	Print button from the Preview screen	File | Print from the Graphs page	145
Print Notebook Pages Separately	Options button from the File Print dialog box or the Preview screen	File | Print	142
Print the Active Page		File | Print	65
Print with Already Created Print Settings		File | Named Settings	
Right-align Headers and Footers	Page Setup button from the Preview screen, then | |	File | Page Setup	143
Save Print Settings		File | Named Settings	140
Set Up the Page to Be Printed		File | Page Setup	
Set Up the Printer		File | Printer Setup	
Zoom In to Preview	Left-click or type [+] from the Preview screen		138
Zoom Out to Preview	Right-click or type [−] from the Preview screen		138

Troubleshooting Guide

WINDOWS

Problem

When you double-click on an icon to start a program, it just moves around the screen.

Solution

You are holding down the mouse button a little too long. Double-click again, holding down the mouse button for the shortest possible time.

Problem

In Windows, a box appears on the screen with the prompt "This will end your Windows session."

Solution

You have attempted to close the Program Manager from the Control menu box. Click on the Cancel button to remain in Windows.

QUATTRO PRO FOR WINDOWS

Problem

You begin entering new data in a cell, which erases existing cell contents.

Solution

If you have not yet pressed [Enter], press [Esc]

Problem

To edit cell contents, you start typing, which erases existing cell contents.

Solution

Press [Esc] to preserve the original cell contents, then press [F2] to enter Edit mode.

Problem

You have selected the wrong block of cells with the mouse.

Solution

Position the mouse on the starting cell again and click. The block will disappear. Then select the correct block of cells. You will find it helpful to drag the mouse slowly to ensure accuracy.

Problem

You have accidentally copied a block of cells to the wrong place.

Solution

If the block is still highlighted, press [Del]. This will delete the cells. If the block is not highlighted, select it. Then press [Del]

Problem

The cell block displays asterisks rather than the correct value.

Solution

Quattro Pro for Windows displays a row of asterisks in a cell whenever a formatted value is too wide for the existing column. Use the Fit button on the SpeedBar or use the Object Inspector menus to widen the column.

Problem	Solution
You want to enter a label consisting of a series of numbers (for example, a zip code, address, or Social Security number), but Quattro Pro for Windows won't display it properly.	If you type a series of numbers, Quattro Pro for Windows assumes you are entering a value. Type an apostrophe (') at the beginning of the series of numbers to let Quattro Pro for Windows know you are typing a label, not a value. The apostrophe will not appear in the cell, but it will appear on the input line when the cell is highlighted.
When trying to enter a function, you see a dialog box with the message "Syntax Error".	You have forgotten to type the closing parenthesis. Click on the OK button on the dialog box and add the closing parenthesis.
You want to change the graph type, but Type is dimmed out on the Graph menu.	In order for you to choose Graph ¦ Type, the graph must be selected. Click on the graph to select it. Then click on Graph ¦ Type.
You want to change graph properties, but you get the wrong menu when you try to call up Object Inspector menus.	Graphs are more complicated than cell blocks. You must be sure that you have positioned the mouse correctly in order to display the correct menu. If you accidentally display the wrong one, click on the Cancel button, reposition the mouse, and try again.
You want to divide the window horizontally into two separate windows, but you get a vertical divider when you click on the Screen Splitter.	You have positioned the mouse on the bottom part of the Screen Splitter rather than on the top. Move the mouse up *slowly* until it changes to the arrow with the horizontal bar.
You want to divide the window vertically into two separate windows, but you get a horizontal divider when you click on the Screen Splitter.	You have positioned the mouse on the top part of the Screen Splitter rather than on the bottom. Move the mouse down *slowly* until it changes to the arrow with the vertical bar.
You want to edit only one page in a group, but you keep editing the other pages at the same time.	You are in Group mode. Click on the Group button to turn it off. Always turn off Group mode when you are finished with the operation that required it.

Index

@

@COUNT Function, 76
@IF Function, 81–82
@MAX Function, 76
@MIN Function, 76
@PMT Function, 77
@SUM Function, 45–46, 59

A

Absolute cell address, 43–45, 79
Absolute cell references, 126
Active page, 22, 65
Add cell contents across grouped pages, 130–131
Add column of cells, 45–46
Add text, 109
Alignment, 73, 143
Alphabetical order, 75, 93
Alt + F3 keystroke, 46, 60, 76–78
Annual payments, 77–78
Apostrophe, 72
Arithmetic symbols, 28
Arrow keys, 2–3, 25, 46
Ascending order, 75, 93
Asterisk, 28

B

Backspace key, 22
Bar graphs, 103
Block
   copy, 40–42
   defined, 39
   delete, 50
   drag and drop, 39–40, 126
   Fill, 89–91
   move, 119, 126
   noncontiguous, 128
   select, 39–40, 72–73
   sequential values, 89–91
   sort, 74
Boldface, 29
Borland, 1
Boxes, drawing, 63–65
Button, 9

C

Cancel, 22
Caps Lock key, 70
Cell
   add across grouped pages, 130
   address, 22, 43–45, 79
   copy, 60–62
   defined, 22
   delete contents, 28
   formulas, 27–28, 42–43
   move, 63
   paste to pages in group, 129
   select cell block, 72–73
Cell selector, 22
Center text on page, 137
Click, 3
Close notebook, 33
Close windows, 9
Column
   add, 45
   delete, 59
   insert, 58
   labels, 144
   scroll bar, 21, 25
   select, 58
   width, 49–50, 71
Combination key commands, 3
Comma format, 73–74
Command summary, 16–17, 34–35, 51, 66–67, 82–83, 98, 114–115, 131–132, 146–147
Conditional statements, 81–82
Context-sensitive, 47
Control menu, 8
Copy
   block, 40–42
   button, 61
   cell contents, 60
   formulas, 61–62
   functions, 61–62, 78–80
   labels, 61
   numbers, 61
Corrections, 22
Count nonblank cells, 76
C prompt, 5
Criteria table, 94
Ctrl key, 41
Ctrl + left arrow keystroke, 25
Ctrl + right arrow keystroke, 25
Currency format, 46, 73–74, 79
Cut button, 63

D

Database
   design, 87–92
   extract records, 95–96
   field names, 91–92
   locate records, 94–95
   Point mode, 97–98
   reset Data | Query, 96–97
   sort, 92–93
Data entry shortcut, 27
Data Query dialog box, 94–97
Data | Sort, 92–93

164 Index

Dates, 143
Default column width, 71
Delete block, 50
Delete cell contents, 28
Delete column, 59
Delete row, 59
Del key, 22
Descending order, 75
Desktop, 6–12
Dialog box, 14, 97
Dimmed commands, 8
Disk, formatting a, 14–15
Disk menu, 14
Disk Operating System (DOS), 4
Division symbol, 28
Dollar sign shortcut, 44, 79
DOS. *See* Disk Operating System
Dots symbol, 40
Double-click, 4, 11
Double-headed arrow, 10
Drag, 4, 39–40, 126
Drag and drop, 39–40, 126

E

Edit cell information, 22, 25–26
Edit field, 14
Edit mode, 26, 43
Edit notebook
    change values, 56–57
    copy cell contents, 60–62
    copy functions, 78–80
    delete rows and columns, 59
    draw lines and boxes, 63–65
    insert columns, 58–59
    insert rows, 57–58
    move cell contents, 63
    print active page, 65–66
    subtotals, 59–60
Edit series, 108–109
Enter data, 26
Enter key, 2
Equal symbol, 28
Esc key, 22
Exit Quattro Pro, 33–34
Exit a Windows program, 19

Exit Windows, 15–16
EXT, 72
Extended mode, 72

F

F2 function key, 26, 43
F3 function key, 46
F4 function key, 44, 79
F7 function key, 72–73
Field, 87, 91–92
File Manager, 12–14
File | Retrieve, 124
Floating graph, 104–105
Footers, 137, 143, 145
Format Comma, 74
Format Currency, 46, 73
Format a disk, 14–15
Format percent, 77
Formulas, 27–28, 42–46, 59–61
Function keys, 2–3
Functions, 45–46, 61, 76–80

G

Graphs
    bar, 103
    create, 102–114
    floating, 104–105
    Graph menu, 106–109
    Graph tool, 103
    headers and footers, 145–146
    line, 102, 110–111
    menu, 102
    name, 110
    print, 104, 114, 145
    rotated, 107
    save, 114
    series, 106–109
    series labels, 111–113
    text, 109
    types, 103–104
    view, 110
Greater than symbol, 28
Group button, 127–128
Grouped pages, 127–130
Group expressions, arithmetic, 28

H

Header font attributes, 139
Header Font button, 139
Headers, 136, 143, 145
Heading, 144
Highest value in block, 76
Home key, 25

I

Icon
    defined, 7
    double-click, 11
    rearrange, 8
    restore window size, 7, 10–11
Input line, 21–22, 27
Insert column, 58–59
Insert row, 57
Italics, 29

K

Kahn, Phillippe, 1
Keyboard, 2–4
Key field, 87

L

Label, 61, 72
Left heading, 144
Less than symbol, 28
Line graphs, 102, 110–111
Lines, draw, 63–65
Links, create, 78
Loan payments, 77–78
Lowest value in block, 76

M

Margins, 139
Maximize, 7, 9–10
Menu, defined, 6
Menu bar, 8–9, 21, 30–31
Menu commands, 30–33
Microsoft (MS), 4
Minimize, 9–10

Minus sign, 28, 138
Modify label, 61
Monthly payment function, 77–78
Mouse
   buttons, 22
   copy, 40–42
   pointer, 7, 40
   select, 39–40
   techniques, 3–4
Move among columns, 25
Move among pages, 23
Move among rows, 25
Move between and within windows, 122–123
Move block between pages, 119–121
Move cell contents, 63
Move cell selector, 23
MS. *See* Microsoft
MS-DOS, 4
Multiple-page notebook
   add cell contents, 130–131
   change page names, 120–121
   divide notebook, 125–127
   File | Retrieve, 124
   group of pages, 127–131
   move block between pages, 119–120
   noncontiguous blocks, 128–129
   preview before printing, 138–140
   print block, 141–144
   print on one page, 135–137
   print settings, 140–141
   SpeedBar buttons, 129
   split screen, 122–124
Multiplication symbol, 28

N

Noncontiguous blocks, 128
Notebook
   block, 39–40
   change values, 56
   close, 33
   copy, 40–42
   create, 38–51
   display new blank, 33
   divide into multiple pages, 125–127
   edit, 55–66
   headings, 144–145
   keyboard select, 72–73
   mouse select, 39–40
   move among pages, 23–24
   multiple-page, 118–131
   open, 55–56
   overview, 22–23
   print, 65
   save, 32. *See also* Edit notebook
Not equal symbol, 28
Numbers. *See* Value
Numeric format, 47
Numeric sort, 93

O

Object Inspector menus, 47–49, 75, 111–113
Open notebook, 55–56
Operating system, 4–5
Output block, 94–96

P

Page
   groups, 127–130
   names, 120–121
   notebook, 22–24
   numbers, 143
   scroll bar, 21, 24
   select, 63
   Setup button, 139
   tabs, 21–24
Page Down key, 25, 46
Page Up key, 25, 46
Paste button, 61, 63
Payment function, 77–78
Percent format, 77
Pie charts, 102
Plus sign, 27, 138
Pointer, 40
Point mode, 97–98
Preview screen, 138–140
Print
   active page, 65–66
   center text, 137
   graphs, 104–105, 114, 145–146
   headings, 144–145
   multiple-page block, 141–144
   multiple-page notebook on one page, 135–137
   notebook pages separately, 142
   preview, 138–140
   settings, 140–141
Program group, 6
Program Manager, 7

Q

Quarterly payments, 77–78
Quattro Pro, exit, 33–34
Quattro Pro, start, 20–22

R

Rearrange icons, 8
Record, 87, 94–96
Relative cell address, 43–45
Reset button, 97
Reset Data | Query, 96–97
Resize windows, 123–124
Restore window size, 7, 10–11
Return key, 2
Right-click, 3
Rotated graph, 107
Row
   delete, 59
   insert, 57–58
   labels, 144
   scroll bar, 21, 25
   select, 57

S

Save graphs, 114
Save notebook, 32
Schmitz, Ruth, 5
Screen Splitter, 122–124
Scroll bars, 13, 24

Index

Select All button, 21
Select block, 72–73
Select column, 58
Select page, 63
Select row, 57
Sequential values, 89–91
Series, 106–109
Shift + F7 keystroke, 72–73
Single-headed arrow, 10
Sort block, 74
Sort database, 92–93
SpeedBar, 21, 28–29, 49–50, 57–59, 61–62, 129
SpeedSort, 74–75
SpeedSum, 45, 130
SpeedTab button, 21, 24
Splitting screen, 122–124
Spreadsheet Print Options dialog box, 142
Start program, 12–14
Start Quattro Pro, 20–22
Start value, 90
Start Windows, 6
Step value, 90
Stop value, 90
Subtotal, 59–60

T

TAB key, 32
Text, center on printed page, 137
Text, graph, 109
Title bar, 9, 21, 31
Top heading, 144

V

Value
    change, 46–49, 56–57
    defined, 26
    highest, 76
    lowest, 76
    sequential, 89–91
    start, 90
    step, 90
    stop, 90. *See also* Formulas; Functions

W

Width, column, 49–50, 71
WIN command, 6

Windows
    close, 9
    desktop, 6–12
    exit, 15–16
    keyboard, 2–4
    move between, 122–123
    move within, 122
    open, 9
    overview, 4–5
    resize, 7, 9–11, 123–124
    restore, 7, 10–11
    start, 6
Words. *See* Label

X

X-axis series, 106

Y

Y-axis series, 106

Z

Zoom in, 139
Zoom level, 138
Zoom out, 139